# A Critical Analysis of Vijay Tendulkar's

# Kanyadaan

## Dr. Beena A. Mahida

**CANADIAN**
Academic Publishing

2014

Price : $27.86

First Edition : December, 2014

ISBN :    978-1-926488-19-6

ISBN Allotment Agency : Library and Archives Canada (Govt. of Canada)

Published & Printed by
Canadian Academic Publishing
81, Woodlot Crescent,
Etobicoke,
Toronto, Ontario, Canada.
Postal Code- M9W 6T3
Phone- +1 (647) 633 9712
http://www.canadapublish.com

# PREFACE

Indian Drama has undergone various metamorphoses after independence Drama in regional Language are still popular in the midst of Multiplexes, because it is a means of spreading morality and entertainment. After all it is one of the branches of Fine Arts Which gives pleasure as well reflects life in its various shades. In regional drama the contemporary Indian Dramatists Mohan Rakesh, Girish Karnard and Badal Sircar are well known in Marathi Drama Late Vijay Tendulkar is ranked as a Frontline Playwright in the Contemporary Indian Theatre.

Drama in India has a long history and in regional languages it is as popular as other literary genres – fiction and poetry. In Indian Literature, drama in English has not attained much popularity because plays in regional languages dominate the theatre. In recent times, Plays in the regional languages are translated in to English and such translations have established link between East and West, and North and South as well as harmony and unity in modern India.

In this context Vijay Tendulkar's Marathi Plays occupy a unique place. When I read the English translation of Tendulkar's plays I decided to pursue my research on plays of Tendulkar and in this decision Dr.R.K.Madalia of the Department of English provided much needed help by accepting to become my Supervisor for the research. He suggested to carry out my research on Tendulkar's major 6 (six) plays and to analyse them from the point of view of characterization, themes and dramatic techniques. Each of the plays of Tendulkar presented new perspective which made stimulating reading.

Tendulkar has not contributed to the modern Marathi theatre but has given it a new dimension. His plays disturb the audience by raising complex issues that remain unsettled even today in modern India. Tendulkar is not feminist but women are at the center in his plays. He treats his women characters with understanding and compassion against men who are selfish and hypocritical.

I have tried my level best in analyzing the different aspects of Tendulkar's Plays yet I believe that literature offers vast spectrum and if something is left out in my research, I leave it to future scholars to pursue studies that are more elaborate. This book is slight modification of the thesis. I have separated each play for a separate book to get wider information regarding the play and the details within and tried to focus in details the themes, characters, and important aspects.

The present book deals with Tendulkar's play Kanyadaan. Kanyadaan includes themes like class differences and caste conflict in modern India as well as the problem of marital relations in the Patriarchal Society through the Characters of Jyoti, Mr.Nath and Arun . The journey in giving shape to this book taught me a lot specially have discovered new canvas of Tendulkar. "Kanyadaan, is the most controversial play of Vijay Tendulkar. It deals with extremely sensitive social and political issue, namely, the conflict between the upper caste (Savarna) and Dalits, a phenomenon still rampantly prevalent in several parts of India."

The success or failure of any work of art depends upon its appeal – whether that appeal proves to be transitory or everlasting. A work of art with an everlasting appeal always remains eternal. It will not be out of the way or excessive exaggeration if the same thing is said about Tendulkar's plays.

**Dr. Beena A. Mahida**

# CONTENTS

# 1. INTRODUCTION

Art is inevitable part of human culture. Art is knowledge coupled with emotions. Human interest in art has been eternal and this eternity has made man civilized and cultured. Art is concerned with expression and man expresses himself through any form of art.

In literary criticism art is divided into two types. Fine Arts and other than Fine Arts. The function of fine arts is to afford pleasure while other arts satisfy human needs. Architecture, sculpture, music and poetry are fine arts. Drama is included in Fine arts. Other literary forms find expression in statement but drama finds expression in acting. Compared to other literary forms drama is very close to human life hence it is said "Drama makes the spectators hearts dance" Drama is said to be the mirror of the world because on its small scale the full context of human life is revealed. It is a process that originates in the writer's mind and completes itself when it touches the heart of the spectators. It is a world of make-believe and its roots are in performance.

Drama has always remained a unique means to spread morality and to entertain. Long before movies came into being Indian theatre had been a major source of spreading moral value and entertainment. The remarkable feature is that- in spite of the emergence of the Indian cinema, the Indian theatre has not lost significance.

The Indian cinema with all its advanced techniques, sophisticated cameras and freedom of variety has remained unsuccessful in surpassing the Indian Theatre. No doubt – an actor who works in a cinema gets more money than a player of the stage but- the player of the stage gets more appreciation than the actor on the screen. The camera of a movie allows the compensation of a re-take to the actor whereas for the artist of a theatre no re-take is possible. His work demands more sincerity and higher efficiency which finally bring greater appreciation to him.

The tradition of Indian Drama is very old. It goes back to the Sanskrit Drama of ancient India. India being a large country with diverse cultures and regional languages has various traditions of form and matter, distinct and yet having many common factors of dramaturgy. Modern Indian drama is influenced not only by classical Sanskrit drama or local folk forms but also by western theatre following the establishment of British rule in India.

**N. S. Dharan**, an eminent writer of Indian writing in English writes "Drama in India has a long history". Girish Karnad says that the earliest extant play in India was written as early as A.D. 200. Dating to the days of Bhasa, Bhavabuti and Kalidasa, drama can boast of a rich and chequered history. The early plays were written in Sanskrit, based on the Vedas and the Upanishads. In fact, the Vedas and the Upanishads have never ceased to be sources of inspiration to man of letters both in India and abroad. Down the centuries, Indian drama has undergone various metamorphoses and it still continues to flourish in all regional languages. In regional languages it enjoys almost an equal status along with two other major literary genres, namely fiction and poetry. In Indian literature drama in English is yet to register an appreciable growth. By and large, plays written in regional languages dominate the Indian theatre. These plays are easily intelligible to the audiences. Actors too can easily improvise in them.

Several regional amateur theatres have also flourished from time to time. In the post-Independence period, performing arts were employed as an effective means of public enlightenment during the First-Five year plan (1951-54). As a result the National school of Drama was established under the directorship Alkhazi. Institutions for training in dramatics were founded in big cities. Drama departments started functioning in several universities. The annual Drama Festival was started in New Delhi by the Sangit Natak Akademi in 1954. With so much encouragement coming from so many quarters, drama began to flourish in the regional languages.

During the last few years, several plays, originally written in the regional languages, have been translated into English. Today, a sizeable number of such plays do exist. According to many academicians, it is necessary to incorporate these translations into the corpus of Indian English Literature as they also contribute an important component to it. Such translations of plays have forged an effective link between the East and the West the North and the South of India and contributed, in no small measure, to the growing harmony and richness of contemporary creative consciousness.

According to **Indranath Chaudhary**, when the sahitya Akademi was set up in 1954, Dr. S. Radhakrishnan spelt out its objective as the promotion of the unity of Indian literature, despite India's geographical, political, Social, and Linguistic diversities. Dr. Radhakrishnan gave a slogan to the Akademi that Indian literature is one, though written in many languages. It is in this context that the plays of Girish Karnad in Kannada, Mohan Rakesh in Hindi, Badal Sircar in Bengali and Vijay Tendulkar in Marathi occupy a unique place as pointed out by **Arundhati Banerjee** :

"In the 1960s four dramatisls from different regions of India writing in their own regional languages were said to have ushered modernity in to the sphere of Indian drama and theatre. They were Mohan Rakesh in Hindi, Badal Sircar in Bengali and Vijay Tendulkar in Marathi and Girish Karnad in Kannada.

Rakesh's untimely death left his life's work incomplete, and Karnad has written only intermittently. Sircar, of course, has been almost as active as Tendulkar though his plays can be divided in to three distinct periods. Tendulkar, however, has not only been the most productive but has also introduced the greatest variations in his dramatic creations."

**V. B. Deshpande** rightly states, "Since the Independence – since 1950, to be precise – the name of Vijay Tendulkar has been in the forefront of the Marathi drama and stage. His personality both as man and writer is multifaceted. It has often been puzzling and curious with a big question mark on it. In the last 55 years he has written stories, novels, one – act plays, plays for children as well adults. Similarly he has done script6 writing and news paper columns as well. And in all these fields he has created an image of his own. Thus he is a creative writer with a fine sensibility and at the same time a contemplative and controversial dramatist. He has made a mark in the field of journalism also. Because of his highly individual viewpoint and vision of life and because of his personal style of writing he has made a powerful impression in the field of literature and drama, and has given the post-independence, Marathi drama a new idiom. By doing this he has put Marathi drama on the national and international Map."

The same indebtedness is expressed by **Arundhati Banerjee** "Vijay Tendulkar has been in the vanguard of not just Marathi but Indian theatre for almost forty years".He not only pioneered the experimental theatre movement in Marathi but also guided it."

While talking about contemporary Marathi Theatre **Dhyaneshwar Nadkarni** points out,

"Vijay Tendulkar leads the vanguard of the avant garde theatre that developed as a movement separate from the mainstream. Tendulkar and his colleagues were dissatisfied with the decadent professional theatre that characterized the Thirties and Forties. They wanted to give theatre a new form and therefore experimented with all aspects of it including content, acting décor and audience communication."

**Chandrasekhar Barve** expresses a similar opinion about Tendulkar's contribution to Marathi theatre,

"We can say with certainty that Tendulkar has guided Marathi drama that seemed to have lost its proper track, and has kept leading it for over two decades. His place and importance in this respect shall remain unique in the history of Marathi drama. There may be controversies regarding his greatness but his achievements are beyond question.

He has written 28 full length plays, 24 one-act plays, several middles, articles, editorials and 11 plays for children. In spite of his success in every genre, his versatility as a writer has been overshadowed by his fame as a dramatist since drama has been his forte.

**Mr. Barve observes,**

"His extra-dramatic writing also reveals his pure taste for drama which tries to capture the different tensions and through them, finds "dramatics" accurately".His one-act plays are more experimental than his full-length plays. Most of them have been translated and produced in major Indian languages and some of them into English.

Vijay Tendulkar was born in **1928** at **Bombay** in **Maharastra**. He was born and brought up in Kandevali, a small lane in Girgaon. A lower middle class community dwelt. There and the males were mostly the shopkeepers and clerks. He was living in a typical chawl, in apartments of one room, kitchen, balcony and common toilets, so Tendulkar's upbringing in a lower middle class community provided him chance to perceive middle class minutely which helped him to portray its different shades on the stage.

His **father Mr. Dhondopant Tendulkar** was a head clerk at a British publishing firm called Longmans Green and company (Now Orient Longman). His **mother Mrs. Susheela Tendulkar** was a housewife. His father was a writer, director and actor of amateur Marathi plays. He didnot join the commercial drama company as formerly a career in the theatre was not honoured. Four years old Tendulkar used to go with his father to the rehearsals so he nurtured love for the theatre from his childhood. Tendulkar himself considers those rehearsals as a kind of "Magic show". Because like magic he saw the living beings change into characters. He saw with wonder the male performing the roles of woman by changing their voice and movements. He didn't have any exposure to other theatre except what his father staged.

Tendulkar had other **brother** named **Raghunath** and **sister Leela**. His two elder sisters died in infancy. He had two younger brothers but- he was the favourite child of his parents. He was sickly child and suffering from cough and asthmatic wheezing. So special care, protection and love were provided to this sickly boy by the parents for fear of losing him if not protected well. He was given the **pet name "Papia"** and above all he was known as a **"Mother's child"** being favourite of his mother. Emotionally he was more attached with his mother than his father. He remembers how his mother used to feed him forcefully.

Due to his unhealthy body the family servant used to take him to school. It was municipal school. As usual it had small dingy rooms with awful toilets and it had no playground and water at times. In the school also special attention was given to him as he belonged to somewhat well to do family. His teachers used to borrow story books from him and by becoming partial they left him alone at the examination. Thus he studied in an average Indian school, which has no basic facilities but he carries those moments in comparison with sophisticated school where he studied later in life. At 9 years of age he attended "Chikisaha samooha", where he found himself totally strange among the sophisticated children and spacious buildings.

Tendulkar surprisingly started his career as a **writer** at a very early stage of life. He wrote stories and essays when he was **6** years of age. His father was a writer, director and actor so creativity was inborn in him. The unpublished work of his father lay at home and little Tendulkar passed his time with books and had read novel and short stories of eminent writers so he grew up in a literary atmosphere. The seed had already been sown in little mind for literature and gradually it took the shape of huge tree.

He had never imagined himself to be a writer in his childhood. As a small child he wanted to be an engine driver or an acrobat in circus and dreamt of wondering from place to place astonishing the crowd by daredevil acts. He used to visit fairs and circus with his father which were like big fairyland for him. So childlike curiosity, interest and amazement surrounded him along with his keen interest in reading. Sunday and vacation had special attraction for him. On Sunday morning his father used to take him to a large bookshop of his friend used to buy books of his choice. In evening his father took him to chowpatty beach and they travelled in train from Charni Road to Colaba which attracted him a lot. During summer vacation the family used to go for Goa or to Port Ratnagiri.

Tendulkar remembers that his father was a strict disciplinarian, impractical, stubborn but an honest man. "To be honest is a disqualification in todays world" and so Mr. Dhondopant Tendulkar never got the honour of being honest and idealist. He never took bribes or extra fees. But he felt proud to be poor and was very much content with life. Due to this the later life of his father was miserable. The elder brother Raghunath quarrelled with him and left the home. His father was against the dowry system and so Tendulkar's sister Leela didn't get married and had to remain single. It seems that the father had never got family love due to certain principles.

Apart from the influence of the father, Raghunath, his brother also played formative influence on Tendulkar. His brother was a follower of Gandhi and Gandhian principles. He used to attend political congress meetings. The father wanted him to be active in studies but he went astray. He wanted to marry Hansa Wadkar which was unbearable for the idealist father and so the family separated from Raghunath and moved to Kolhapur. Tendulkar used to get gifts like pastries, sweets and pen from his brother. He used to go for English movies with his brother. But his brother died miserably due to alchoholic habit.

The later childhood of Tendulkar passed at Kolhapur – a princely state in Maharastra. At Kolhapur he made himself noticeable by his excellence in reciting English poems. When he was **11 years** old, he **wrote** and **directed** and **acted "Maya Bazaar".** This way, the journey of this veteran writer towards performing arts started. At Kolhapur his friend was the son of one prominent playwright named Na vi kulkarni, who shared the same literary interest with Tendulkar. He even worked as a **child artist** in **two Marathi** Films.

As a teenager, at the **age** of **13** the family shifted to Pune and he attended a new school. He believed that he might have completed matriculation but the **Quit India Movement** was in momentum and Tendulkar was one of those who obeyed Gandhi's call to boycott the school. He started taking part in campaign against Britishers and he used to attend the early morning meetings without informing his parents. At the **age** of **14** while attending such meeting, he **was arrested** and the family came to know about Tendulkar's active participation in freedom fighting. Again he attended the school but now he started bunking the classes and developed the habit of spending the monthly fees of the **school** in watching English films. The visuals had a good impact on him. This exposure to the theatre at an early age has had its strong influence on him as a **successful** dramatist. He says in an interview, "As a school boy I had watched the Hollywood films playing in my hometown, not once, but each one over and over again. I still remember the visuals, not the dialogues which I didn't understand. A more conscious education in what the visual could do came when I worked with the Rangayan Theatre group in Bombay, but watching Marcel Marceau from the last seat in the last row was an enthralling experience. Not a single word was uttered, but so much was expressed. After that I wrote mimes for quite a while. I felt the visual had unlimited possibilities, the word was useless. But I am a playwright, words are my tools, I had to use them." Apart from Films he denoted his time at the city library in reading which helped him a lot during his career as a journalist. But his father was disappointed seeing the poor prospect of Tendulkar.

At Pune, Tendulkar found the **Role Model** of his life –
**Dinkar BalKrishna Mokashi,** a radio mechanic but a good writer.
He led a very simple life and Tendulkar was impressed by his
personality and the informality of his writing style. His other **Role
Model** was **Vishnu Vinayak Bokil,** a teacher and a writer.
Tendulkar liked his light hearted, jovial and exuberant style. He
remembered one incident of the school when Mr. Vinayak asked
the students to look at the names of rank holders of the school on
the board and asked, "Where are those top rankers now? Does
anyone know?"Then he said that the students should pass the exam
as the parents pay the fees but the marks they get were not
everything. He advised them to develop their personality in other
directions also. It worked as a boosting to the teen Tendulkar to
look beyond the school. Later on, as a writer Tendulkar dedicated
one of his book to this school teacher Mr. Vinayak.

**At 16**, Tendulkar **left the school** for good. He had no
friends and no any communication with his parents. He wanted to
talk! But with whom! He had to talk with himself! And he put all
his dialogues with his own self on paper through various forms-
poems stories, film scripts and at this stage of his life his writing
acquired a conscious motivation.

At the age of **22** he wrote his **First full length original
play "Grihastha"** which flopped like anything and he took an oath
that he would never write a play in life and to his surprise he has
written **28 full length** plays as well as he has been **working
actively** in the theatre world for the last **45 years.**

He always considers himself a writer first and a playwright after words. About his love for writing he writes,

"The point is more than a playwright, I consider myself to be a writermeaning I loved to indulge in the physical process of writing. I enjoy this process even when there is nothing to be said. Give me a piece of paper any paper and pen and I shall write as naturally as a bird flies or a fish swims. Left to myself, I scribble. And I never get tired of writing… Especially when I write in my mother tongue i.e. Marathi. Writing gives me a pleasure which has no substitute. However, tired I am physically or mentally, the moment I pick up the pen and begin running it on a paperany piece of paper I feel good I feel refreshed I feel as if I am born again. Writing by itself is a luxury for me. When I write, I forget myself, I forget my anxieties…"

He has been writing in different roles by using different mediums. He was **journalist**. He had been **sub-editor** and executive editor in journals and assistant editor of a daily. He used to write editorials with the information received from the second hand sources. This filled him with great dissatisfaction. He says,

"It started with my journalistic dissatisfaction but it grew into much bigger proportions in the sense that it became a matter of conscience as a human being. I became restless."

The violence, the oppression and the exploitation in the society that he witnessed made him restless. And journalism could not offer him a viable solution for his mental agitation. But it does shape his dramatic career. **Gowri Ramnarayan**, therefore points out: "With his exposure to Marathi theatre from childhood, and journalistic background Vijay Tendulkar turned contemporary socio-political situations into explosive drama."

His desire was to start a daily newspaper column and he enjoyed **writing a column** for **six months** in 1993, when Babri Masjid was destroyed. And during those six months he didn't write anything but only enjoyed column writing. He well remembered that during his journalistic days he sometimes wrote for astrology column, when the 'official' astrologer did not reach in time and he enjoyed in forecasting bright future for the unknown readers of the column. As a writer he found good fun in playing the **role** of **an astrologer**.

Being versatile he can put himself in any role. During the period of struggle he did **Ghost writing** with full knowledge that his name would not appear and become known to the readers. He took it as a role with its own "character". His inner personality as a writer underwent a natural change to suit the role. Along with his job in a newspaper he started writing short story and play and even Ghost writing for additional income. His writing developed according to the demands of the roles. He also worked as a **Public Relation Officer** in an industry and wrote copy for add-agencies. He **translated** American Books for the united information services and wrote **scripts** for non-descript Government Documentaries. He played different roles in order to earn his livelihood but his writing practice has brought perfection in writing skill.

Vijay Tendulkar, as a sensitive, sensible and responsible citizen, could not quieten his agitated conscience with his journalistic career. So he left journalism when he received Nehru Fellowship for the 1973-75. During this period, he travelled extensively throughout India and saw directly all kinds of violence. **From this experience, he infers:**

"Unlike communists I don't think that violence can be eliminated in a classless society, or, for that matter, in any society. The spirit of aggression is something that the human being is born with. Not that it's bad. Without violence man would have turned into a vegetable."So he perceived both the positive and negative faces of violence.

Regarding ideology he says,

"I do not align myself to any political ideology.......I do have my sympathies with the left"He does not subscribe to any ideology in his plays. Nor does he write for commercial purpose.

Moreover, in the words of **Mr. Barve,**

"Tendulkar's plays helped to refine Marathi drama that was so far polluted by propaganda for political awakening and social reforms, cheap and vulgar entertainment". Tendulkar does not subscribe to any particular political Ideologies, as they, including Marxism, are unable to understand the complex human situation and to suggest any viable solution to our Hydra-headed problems. Yet he does not lack political awareness.

He says to **Gowri Ramnarayan** in an interview,

"I had a political background, I was involved in the 1942 movement.Journalism developed my political sense, curiosity for instance ………naturally this got in my writing."

He was actively associated with civil liberties movements in Maharashtra. All this shows his great concern for his country and society. He is a realist and refuses to be fooled by romantic concepts of reforms and movements. He exposed the flaws and the inevitable failure of unrealistic reforms and movements in his plays.

Mr. Tendulkar considers himself as an **actor-writer** and himself acted on the stage during his apprentice days in the theatre but did not find it as exciting as writing. He was an actor on the stage of his creative mind. According to him he acts as he writes in his mind he emotes the **lives** of the character as he writes. They are not written words but a total and spontaneous expression of the mind and the personality of the character which includes not only the words but also the eloquent silence in between the words-broken sentences, the subtle emphasis on certain words, even the pitch of the voice, the gestures of the hands. He can 20 visualize the position of the characters on the stage – the total composition of the scene and even the lighting. Thus he acted their speech, behavior patterns and their ways of looking at things. So he believes he can act better than others because he has acted his play out when he wrote the play. **Mr. Tendulkar** was basically **a man of theatre**, which he had inherited from his father and eldest brother. He had a curiosity for this performing art and subconscious and unquenched desire to explore the magic and beauty of this form. His love for the theatre continued as he wrote plays at school, acted in plays, watched it, discussed it and for the last 45 years he was in the world of theatre. He believes that performing art is addictive.

He writes,

"You can learn the "grammar" but art is not mere grammar. It is an expression it provides endless learning by experiments, by committing mistakes."

He remembered that at a very early stage of his life he had developed curiosity for people and consciously noted the speech habits of people, their manners and personal peculiarities. He gives an expression to it in his writing so some of his characters are related to certain living persons. He believed that the creative process is complicated process. The characters would appear in utter chaos till he conceives it. He could never write a play with only idea or theme in mind but he needed character first with him.

He writes,

"I could not proceed to write a play unless I saw my characters as real life people, unless I could see them moving doing things by themselves, unless I heard them emoting, talking to each other, I was never able to begin writing my play only with an idea or a theme in mind. I had to have my characters first with me ........" Thus, they are not puppets but living persons of distinction.

About the structuring of his play he said he had never attended any courses for this skill but he had learnt it by trial and error method which is very costly. He wrote that one has to own money in experimental theatre. No one sponsors the play and by the time the players correct the mistakes they are doing the last show of the play. For him, the Rehearsal Hall had become the learning ground. In absence of theatrical devices the inner mechanism of a play with its positive and negative points were laid open and he learnt a lot from these brain- storming rehearsal sessions. Apart from experimenting in the theatre, watching rehearsals he used to see play every day once, twice or thrice in one day. He did not bother whether the play is good or bad but it helped him in internalizing the techniques of playwriting – especially the structuring of the play.

He learnt a lot by watching films because a film also has to have a structure. Even the **concerts** of **classical music impressed** him though he did not know its grammar but classical music has its strict rules and regulations. The **reading** of **the poems** also supplied him the knowledge about compact structure and a form. The visit to the **Art Galleries** made him aware about the rhythm, form and structure in good painting. Apart from all these **Peter Brook's** Book (Master Craftsman in the art of Theatre) taught him the foremost principles of theatre world that all visual art including the art of the theatre, have one thing in common- The space, and it is the skill of the dramatist that how meaningfully and ingeniously he fills the space.

**Arundhati Banerjee** says,

"Tendulkar's first major work that set him apart from previous generation Marathi playwrights was *Manus Navache Bel ( An Island called Man)* (1955). His dramatic genius was cutout for the newly emerging, experimental Marathi theatre of the time. His direct association with Rangayan at this point of his career and continous interaction with such theatre personalities as Vijaya Mehta, Arvind and Sulabha Despande, Kamalakar Sarang Madhav Vatve and Damoo Kenkre provided new impetus for creative faculties. Thus Manus Navache Bel was closely followed by a spate of plays (1958). *Madhlya Bhinti (The walls Between) Chimnicha Ghar Hota Menacha (Nest of wax) (1958) Mee Jinklo Mee Harlo (I won, I lost) (1963) Kavlanchi Shala (school for crows) (1963) and Sari Ga Sari (Rain o Rain) (1964)* which would chart the course of avant-grade Marathi theatre during the next few years. There seems to be a consistency of theme and treatment in them despite the apparently desperate nature of their subjects. In all these early plays, Tendulkar is concerned with the middle class individual set against the backdrop of a hostile society."

Most of Tendulkar's plays are in the naturalistic writing. However, his Ghashiram Kotwal is in the folk tradition while his last two plays *Niyatioya Bailala (To Hell with Destiny)* and *Safar (The Tour)* emplay fantasy. The play **"Silence! The court is in session"** (1967) made him the centre of a general controversy. He has already been called the angry young man of the Marathi theatre. He was considered a rebel against the established values of a fundamentally orthodox society **Encounter in** Umbugland (1974) is a political allegory (1971) **The Vultures** shocked the conservative sections of Marathi people with its naturalistic display of cupidity, sex, and violence. **Sakharam Binder** (1972) is probably Tendulkar's most intensely naturalistic play and shocked the conservative society even more than **The Vultures**. In **Ghashiram Kotwal** (1972) he moves from the naturalistic writing in to the folk tradition, it explains the power game that are found in Indian politics. **Kamala** (1981) is based on **a** real life incident reported in The Indian Express by Ashwin sarin. Kanyadaan is also one of the controversial play and branded as anti – Dalit play. It actually tries to show how our romantic idealism fails.

He wrote his plays in Marathi, First, he influenced Marathi theatre and guided it. Later, his impact extended to other Indian languages as his plays were translated into them. Tendulkar perceived the realities of the human society without any reconceived notions, reacted to them as a sensitive and sensible human being and wrote about them in his plays as a responsible writer. He never wrote to win a prize or an award.

He says,

"I have written about my own experience and about what I have seen in others around me. I have been true to all this and have not cheated my generation. I did not attempt to simplify matters and issues for the audience when presenting my plays, though that would have been easier occupation. Sometimes my plays jolted society out of its stupor and I was punished. I faced this without regrets. It is an old habit with me to do what I am told not to do. My plays could not have been anything else. They contain my perceptions of society and its value and I cannot write what I do not perceive".

In his plays he deals with the issues of gender inequality, social inequality, power games, self alienation, sex and violence. His characters are very much real. They are neither completely good nor completely bad. He liberated Marathi stage from the tyranny of conventional theatre with its mild doses of social and political satire for purpose of pure entertainment.

**Mr. M. Sarat Babu** writes,

"Vijay Tendulkar portrays the contemporary society and the predicament of man in it with a special focus on the morbidity in his plays, which remind us of Nietzche's words "the disease called man" and also Freud's description of human civilization as "a universal neurosis". His plays touch almost every aspect of human life in the modern world and share the disillusionment of the post modern intellectuals, however they seem to highlight three major issues : gender, power and violence."

Vijay Tendulkar devoted his life for the world of theatre as he says ,

"What I like about those years is that they made me grow as a human being. And theatre which was my major concern has contributed to this in a big way. It helped me to analyse my own life and the lives of others. It led me to make newer and newer discoveries in the vast realm of the human mind which still defies all available theories and logic. It is like an everintriguing puzzle or a jungle which you can always enter but has no way out…"Such a prolific and versatile writer has been felicitated with many awards and honours like

1. The Maharashtra State Government Award ( 1956, 1969 and 1973)

2. The Sangeet Natak Akademi Award (1971)

3. The Filmfare Award (script writer) (1980,1983)

4. The Padmabhushan (1984)

5. The Saraswati Samman (1993)

6. The Kalidas Samman (1999)

7. The Maharashtra Gaurav Puraskar (1999)

8. The Jansthan Award (1999)

9. Katha Chudamani Award (2001)

This legendary theatre man passed away on **19th May, 2008**. He was suffering from Myasthenia Gravis, a neuromuscular disease. He died at the age of 80 in a private hospital at Pune where he was hospitalized since 10th April, 2008.Shirish Prayag, Director of Prayag Hospital stated,"At the time of his demise he was extremely calm and quiet. There was an expression of contentment on his face. His face did not reflect any pain."

Mr. Prayag stated that the family members had discussed the possibility of eye donation but it was decided that since Tendulkar had not expressed such a wish it would be improper to do so. Tendulkar who was in Pune, since he was last discharged from hospital had refused to go back to Mumbai."

According to his wish his last rites were performed at the Vaikanth electric crematorium and prominent theatre and film personalities including Mohan Agashe, Satish Alekar, Haider Ali, Amruta Subhash, Amol Palekar and Atul Pethe, university of Pune vice-chancellor Narendra Jadhav paid last tribute to Tendulkar at the crematorium.

➤ **Condolence Messages on Vijay Tendulkar's DeathPresident Pratibha Patil** said in her condolence message "Vijay Tendulkar was not only an acknowledged figure in Indian literature but also helped Marathi and all of Indian theatre attain recognition at the international level."

➤ **Prime Minister Manmohan** Singh in a condolence message to Tendulkar's family said, "his strog espousal of women's empowerment and the empowerment of the downtrodden has shaped public consciousness in post independence India."

➤ **Leader of Opposition L K Advani** also paid glowing tributes to Tendulkar. He said the playwright was an outstanding writer who gave Marathi theatre a national and international profile."His place, many of which were translated into Hindi and other Indian Languages, were both creative and carried a strong social message,"

- **Maharashtra Chief Minister Vilasrao Deshmukh** also condoled the death of eminent playwright Vijay Tendulkar.In his condolence message, Deshmukh said: "The nation has lost the literary genius and dramatist par excellence. With Tendulkar's death an eventful era has come to an end."

- Noted film **director Shyam Benegal** said : "Tendulkar was one of the greatest playwright of Indian theatre in the last 50 years. Tendulkar wrote screenplay of my films "Nishant" and "Manthan". I respected his creativity and admired him as a human being." "He was a senior professional form our field and his contribution to the Indian theatre was immense," Benegal added.

- **Film director Govind Nihlani** said : "Tendulkar brought modernity to Marathi theatre. He pioneered a paradigm shift in the vision of looking at society and reflecting it through theatre and cinema."

- **Bollywood superstar Mr. Amitabh Bachchan** said : " Vijay Tendulkar was a strong and fearless writer and a great mind. I am deeply saddened to hear the news of his passing away." Amitabh was full of admiration for the man who re-wrote many rules of stage writing. "In today's world it is difficult and though to take a committed stand and pursue it. Vijay Tendulkarji did. And that was his strength. At times this stand is the solitary voice of reason often misunderstood but seldom wrong."

➢ **Amol Palekar said**: "His death is a loss to theatre and literature. wonder whether this losss will ever be recovered. I am glad I could do my share of archiving his entire body of work for the younger generation when my wife Sandhya Gokhale and I organized a Ten Festival in 2006 which went on for a week.

**List of Vijay Tendulkar's Works :**

**One Act :**

Thief Police

Ratra Ani Itar Ekankika (1957)

Chitragupta, Aho Chitragupta (1958)

Ajgar Ani Gandharv (1966)

Bhekad Ani Itar Ekankika (1969)

Ekekacha

Andher Nagari

**Collection of Stories :**

Kaachpatre (1957)

Dwandwa (1961)

Gane (1966)

Phulpakharu (1970)

**Essays :**

Kovil Unhe (1971)

Rat Rani (1971)

Phuge Savanache (1974)

Ram Prakar (1994)

**Children's Plays :**

Ithe Bale Miltat (1960)

Patlachya Poriche Lageen (1965)

Chimna Bandhto Bangla (1966)

Chambhar Chauksiche Natak (1970)

**Novels :**

Kadambari

Katha Eka Vyathechi : Henry James

Nave Ghar : Nave Ayushya : Grace Jordan

Prempatre : Henry James

Aage Barho : G L Letham (1958)

Gele Te Divas (1958)

Devanchi Manse

Amhu Harnhar Nahi: L E Wilder

Ranphul : S L Arora (1963)

Chityachya Magawar : W W Tiberg

Clarke (1957)

## Humour :

Karbhareen : Doroothy Von Doren

## Biography :

Dayechi Devta : H D Wiloston

To Aamchayasathi Ladhla ( Roosevelt) : K O Pear

## Film Script ( Marathi)

Samana
Sinhasan
Umbartha
Akriet
22 June 1897

## Film Script ( Hindi)

Nishant
Manthan
Akrosh
Ardha Satya
Aaghat

| Play | Original Title | Original Author | Original Language | Institution | Director | First Show | Pub. | Yrs. |
|---|---|---|---|---|---|---|---|---|
| Adhe Adhure | Adhe Adhure | Mohan Rakesh | Hindi | Theatre Unit | Satyadev Dube | 11th Jan. 1970 | Popular | 1971 |
| Lincolon Che Akherche Divas | Last Days of Lincolon | Mark Doran | English | - | - | - | Majestic | 1964 |
| Lobh Nasava hi Vinanti | Hasty Heart | John Patrick | English | Rangayan | Arvind Deshpande | - | Parchure | - |
| Tughaluq | Tughaluq | Girish Karnad | Kannda | Avishkar | Arvind Deshpande | 17th Aug. 1971 | Niklanth | 1971 |
| Vasarach Akra | A street Car Named Desire | Tenesse Williams | English | - | - | - | Popular | 1966 |

# Dramatic Works

| Title | Institute | Director | First Show | Publication |
|---|---|---|---|---|
| Ghrihasth (The House Holder) | Mumbai marathi Sahitya Sangha, Drama Wing | Damu Kenkare | 1955 Exact date not known | - |
| Sjro,amt (The rich) | Bharatiya vidya bhavan kala kendra | Vijaya Mehta | 12th Dec. 1955 | 1955 |
| Manus navache Bet (An Island Called man) | Lalit kala Kendra | Damu kenkare | 28th Oct. 1956 | 1956 |
| Madhalya Bhinti (Middle Walls) | Best Art Section | Nandkumar Rawate | 4th Nov. 1958 | 1958 |
| Chimanicha Ghar Hota menacha (The Wax House of the Sparrow | Rangmancha | Vijaya Mehta | 27th Dec. 1959 | 1960 |
| Mi Jinkalo (I Won, I lost) | Rangayan | Vijaya Mehta | 20th Oct. 1963 | 1963 |
| Kavlyanchi Shala (School for Crows) | Rangayan | Vijaya Mehta | 5th Dec. 1963 | 1964 |
| Sarga Sari (Drizzle O Drizzle) | Mumbai Marathi Sahitya Sangh, Drama wing | Arvind Deshpande | 18th May 1964 | 1964 |
| Ek Hatti Mulagi (An obstinate Girl) | Kala Vaibhav | Almram Bhende | 21th Nov. 1966 | 1968 |

| Shatata Court Chalu Ahe (Silence! The Court is in Session) | Rangayan | Arivind Deshpande | 28th Dec. 1967 | 1968 |
|---|---|---|---|---|
| Jhala Anant Hanumant | - | Arvind Deshpande | - | 1968 |
| Dambdwipacha Mukbala (An Encounter in Umbugland) | Rangayan | Arvind Deshpande | 10th Dec. 1969 | 1974 |
| Gidhade (The Vulture) | Theatre Unit | Shriram lagu | 29th May 1970 | 1971 |
| Ashi Pakhare Yeti (So Come Birds) | Progressive Dramatic Association, Pune | Jabbar Patel | 26th Nov. 1970 | 1970 |
| Sakharam Binder | Welcome theatres | Kamalar Sarang | 10th mar. 1972 | 1972 |
| Bhalya kaka | Natya Mandar | Arvind Deshpande | 5th April 1972 | 1974 |
| Gharate Amuche Chan (Nice is our Nest) | Welcome Theatre | kamalakar Sarang | 28th Oct. 1972 | 1973 |
| Ghashiram Kotwal | Progressive Dramatic Association, Pune | Jabbar Patel | 16th Dec. 1972 | 1973 |
| Baby | nateshwar | Kamalakar Sarang | 29th Aug. 1976 | 1975 |
| Bhai Murarrao | Theatre Academy Pune | Mohan gokhale | 13th Sept. 1977 | 1975 |

| Pahije Jatiche | - | Arvind Deshpande | - | 1976 |
|---|---|---|---|---|
| Mitrachi Goshta (A Friend's Story) | Bhumika | Vinay Aapte | 15th Aug. 1981 | 1982 |
| kamala | Kala Rang | kamalakar Sarang | 7th Aug. 1981 | 1982 |
| Kanyadan | INT | Sadashiv Amarapurkar | 12th Feb. 1983 | 1983 |
| Vithala | INT | Sadashiv Amarapurkar | 22nd May 1985 | 1985 |
| Chiranjeev Saubhagya kanshini | Abhishek | Kamalakar Sarang | 14th Dec. 1991 | - |
| Safar | Avishkar | Sulbha Deshpande | 6th Jan. 1992 | - |
| Niyatichya bailala Ho (To Hell with the Bull of the Fate) | - | - | - | - |

## 2.  KANYADAAN : AN OVERVIEW

Kanyadaan (Gift of a Daughter) (1983) is the play for which Vijay Tendulkar was awarded the Saraswati Samman.

But for the same play he was criticised and faced the anger of the audience in the form of Chappal throwing when it was staged in Marathi. The spectators considered it as an anti-dalit play and could not find the main purpose of the playwright. So while receiving the award Tendulkar says "As its creator, I respect both Verdicts."

"Kanyadaan, is the most controversial play of Vijay Tendulkar. It deals with extremely sensitive social and political issue, namely, the conflict between the upper caste (Savarna) and Dalits, a phenomenon still rampantly prevalent in several parts of India."

**Nutan Gosavi** writes in **"Kanyadaan : An expose of political progressives."**

"It is the first major play to be staged after **Ghashiram Kotwal** (1972) and, also as it happens, the last major play of Tendulkar to be staged. If one approaches the play as the successor or to **Ghashiram Kotwal** which, in ways other than merely chronological it is – one is likely to be somewhat disappointed. For here, there is no technical experimentation associated with Ghashiram Kotwal nor does the story of an intercaste marriage seem radical enough. In fact, the play in 1983 with its ambience of the sixties and the seventies looks a sadly dated one. In matters of technique too, Tendulkar has reverted to the discussion plays of the thirties. All in all, an antiquated play, one might exclaim,Tendulkar is flogging the dead horse of the intercaste marriage."

On the other hand, if one looks at the play as the last major one by Tendulkar, he seems to be setting his scores with the detractors of Ghashiram Kotwal, In connection with the earlier play, he had to suffer a lot of Public harassment and humiliation for his alleged attack on the orthodox Poona Brahmins during the Peshwa period. The political radicals, of course had no problems with the play. In fact, they were gleefully delighted by Tendulkar's satire on the Brahmin orthodoxy. The conservatives in their turn had challenged him to write a similar play on the other section of society, and proclaimed that Poona Brahmins, shorn of their age-old eminence and power, were the softest target imaginable. Tendulkar to do him credit, did script a film called "Samana" in which he targeted the co-operative sugar industry, the most powerful political force in Maharashtra. But then the shenanigans of the co-operative sugar barons are far too well known for them to enjoy the iconic status of a Nana Phadnvis and there was no uproar about the film as there was about Ghashiram Kotwal. Now in Kanyadaan, Tendulkar takes on the members of the Poona Brahmin community on to the other side of the political spectrum, as political progressives with socialist leanings. What interests a student of Tendulkar the dramatist is the date of the play, 1983 is a time when, with the impending disintegration of the soviet union and its empire, the Leftist ideology crumbled into the dustbin of history as its internal self-contradictions came to the fore. Now, perhaps, time was ripe to launch an attack on the radicals and their naivette and hypocrisy which were always perceived but not openly pointed out for fear of being termed a reactionary. Tendulkar saw the chance of meeting the challenge thrown at him by the conservatives years before and in the process be with the times, killing, thus, two birds with one stone!"

An over idealistic democratic couple, their revolutionary daughter who marries a down caste poet and gets disillusioned in the consequent turn of events due to the unexpectedly barbaric behaviour of her life partner are presented on stage by Tendulkar with a contemporary relevance." Kanyadaan, is a play with two acts, five scenes and it has limited characters.

As the title suggests, the play centers around marriage. It is an unusual marriage in the sense that it brings in its wake complex problem – problems at once self-created and unforeseen. Jyoti, the daughter of Nath Devalikar, an MLC who insists on democracy at home, has promised to marry Arun Athavali, a Dalit youth. When she informs her parents, her father is ecstatic, but her mother Seva and brother Jayaprakash are unhappy, after they meet Arun and are shocked by his language and behaviour. Arun's excuse for his attitude is the mistreatment meted out to his family and forefathers at the hands of society. Jyoti's decision to marry Arun leads to a crisis which worsens after marriage, as Arun proves to be a violent husband. Around them, the country too, is marching towards Emergency.

At the end, Jyoti is forced to come to terms with her fate as Arun's wife, as she realizes that it is not possible to improve people and change society. Tendulkar has focused on a problem that there is no bridge between the various sections of society and that the attempt to overcome a taboo often leads to greater pitfalls than one can handle.

A close reading of the play reveals that it is written on the two modern trends of literature.

1) Dalit literature

2) Feminism


Through these he discusses

1. The problem of marital relation in the patriarchal society,

2. The class differences and the caste conflict in modern India.

Vijay Tendulkar's short play Kanyadaan which is written-with only sevencharacters, deals with a sensitive social and political issue. As we all know Dalith ssuffer a lot many years in the hands of upper caste people of the society. Tendulkar in this play presents entirely different aspect that the suffering of an upper caste woman and her family in the hands of a Dalith educated young man. He impartially portrays theproblems as they are but not favour any view.

The institution of marriage is unique in the caste based society of India. Hindus give utmost priority to marriage. They take ever thing, for instance caste, character, occupation, economic status etc. into consideration. Of all these things caste of the bride and the bride groom should be the same. If any one of the above is not good usually marriage doesn't take place. In the marriage 'Kanyadaan' is essential feature. It means giving away bride to bridegroom. The title suggests that the play moves around marriage.

# 3. CASTE CONFLICT IN MODERN INDIAN SOCIETY

The first ever reference regarding the varna system is found in the Rigveda, which says

*"brahmno sya mushmasidbahu rajanya krtha*
*uru tadasya yad vaisyah padbhyam sudrah oja."*

(Brahmin becomes his (Purusha's) Mouth, Kshatriyas became Arms , Vishyas became Thais, and Shudras were born out of His legs.)

In the last three decades Dalit literature has become popular and it has spread awarness among the people about the exploitation of the Dalit in one or in another way. Despite 55 years of independence Dalits continue to suffer abject, misery and ill treatment at the hands of the upper castes. Politicians, instead of trying to uproot this evil, seem to capitalize on it. **Dr. Babasaheb Ambedkar's** advice to the writers has become a source of inspiration for Dalit writers. He says –

"I tell very firmly to all writers that spread ideals, and our cultural heritage through your literature. Don't make your ideas narrow instead make it larger…….. you should not forget that in our country one distinguished world exists – the world of downtrodden, neglected people. Try to understand their agony and pain Dedicate your creativity in making their lives dignified through your literature."

These words of Dr. Babasaheb have become a source of inspiration to Dalit writers. The traditional literature deals with kings, princes, the so called people of upper "class" and "caste". In that literature no delineation of the downtrodden is visible. It depicts the "Gods" but not the "Man" who is suppressed, exploited. And today Dalit literature has come forward to give voice of such suppressed, exploited mass of the country.

In our Indian Society due to casteism & class differences the notable personalities like Sambuk, Karn, Aklawaya and Dr. Ambedkar had to suffer and they fought against the evils of the society.

With the passing of time changes have occurred in the society, culture, religion, and literature in India but the complete revolution has not taken palce yet. India has not produced the revolutionists like Karl Marx or Martin Luther. No doubt, Buddha, Phule, Gandhiji, Ambedkar, made a notable contribution in constructing new society. In India still the "Manu" of "Manusmruti" – the originator of class and caste differences is alive in the contemporary India. Still the down-trodden, suppressed group remains "Untouchable" and excluded from the main stream of the society. Their plight continues and so they have taken up the pen to express their agony, their culture, and society.

In literature the saints and writers like Kabir, Raidas, Tukaram, Dadu, Malukm Sahjobai, Nanak, Narsinh Mehta tried to express the "voice" of such down-trodden. In Bhojpuri language Hiradom wrote "Achut ki Shikayat". And that was the first official work of Dalit literature.

Dalit literature originated in the form of revolt against the injustice to the down-trodden people. In Dalit literature, suppressed Man is in the centre and the writer tries to –

- Establish new values & rejects old traditions.
- Establish new society & rejects the caste difference
- Establish new ideology & rejects the rigid thinking.
- Establish the dignified Identity for Dalit
- Advocate – liberty, fraternity, equality
- Advocate that – Dalit is not untouchable but a dignified human being
- Present the true picture of Dalit Society.

Through various forms of literature like novel, drama, poetry the writer gives voice to the agony of the down-trodden.

Vijay Tendulkar is not a Dalit writer but he is always concerned with predicament of human being. He says

"As an individual – or rather as a social being – I feel deeply involved in the existing state of my society ( because I'm affected by it thoug h not immediately in some cases or not as much as some others are) and in my own way brood over it. As a social being. I am against all exploitation and I passionately feel that all exploitation must end."

**About the genesis of "Kanyadaan" Tendulkar writes :**

"All my creative writing begins, not from an idea but from an experience, mine or somebody else's which then becomes mine. It was such an experience of another to begin with, that provided the starting point for Kanyadaan."

In this play Tendulkar presents quietly different themes. Here he does not depict a Dalit character who is exploited by the society or neglected and who wants equality or rights in the society. But Arun Athavale, a young Dalit boy is able to get married to a Brahmin girl of upper class, and treats her as an object of revenge against all the persons of higher caste & class. Here, instead of Dalit person, a girl of higher strata, suffers humiliation, and tortures at the hand of a dalit boy. So many critics believe that instead of arousing sympathy for Dalit, this play produces anti-Dalit feelings.

Actually, Tendulkar does not want to create anti-dalit feeling by presenting its hero Arun Athavale as brutal man but he wants to analyse the psyche of the Dalits. They are so much suppressed by ages that now even if the "Savaran" tries to accept them, they deny the acceptance. Their psyche is disturbed in such a way by the humiliation that, they want to remain "Dalit", "untouchable" and never trust the so called upper caste people, even though chances and opportunities are given. This sad reality of the present day India is depicted by Tendulkar in the play through the love story of Jyoti and Arun. Through the revengeful spirit of Arun, Tendulkar also highlights the exploitation of the Dalit in the past and its effect on the post Independence Indian Dalit. So in a way Tendulkar examines the pre-independent Indian Dalit life and post-independent Indian Dalit life and draws clear cut difference between the two.

The play presents the civilized family of Nath Devlalikar, who is "Gandhivadi" democrat MLC. He is not only preacher of Gandhian philosophy to public but practices it in his own family and observes democracy at home. Like Gandhiji he does not believe in casteism and holds liberal ideas. Critics believe that Nath is none other than Tendulkar himself and as Tendulkar writes –

"Nath Devlalikar, the protagonist of Kanyadaan is me and many other liberals of my generation whom I understand completely. The pain of these people today, the defeat they have suffered, the fundamental confusion and naivete that has led to their pain and defeat, these form the theme of Kanyadaan and I wrote about it because it came so close to me."

Mr. Nath in the opening of the play states to his daughter about his disillusionment regarding independent India, he says –

"The visions we had of the future of this nation before independence! And what we are forced to see today! Disgusting it hurts."

But he advocates ideals, morals at home. He is very friendly with his children Jayprakash and Jyoti and they too follow the Gandhian principles in their lives. So when his daughter Jyoti expresses her desire to get married a Dalit youth – Arun Athavale, he does not feel surprise. On the contrary, he welcomes the liberal idea of his daughter. He says – "I know it doesn't make a difference. But if my daughter had decided to marry into high caste, it wouldn't have pleased me as much ....."

But the mother Seva opposes the very idea of getting married to a dalit boy. Seva is also a socialist & democrat but a realistic woman. She is not blind to implement all the Gandhian philosophy at her home. So she is shocked and firmly resists Jyoti's decision to get married to a dalit. She interrogates Jyoti about Arun, his family background and his job. When she comes to know that Jyoti is acquainted with him for the last two months she thinks that Jyoti has taken the decision in haste. When she finds that Nath is supporting Jyoti in her reforming idea, being realist she tries to persuade Jyoti. And actually her persuasion presents the theme of the play. She says –

"My anxiety is not over his being a dalit. You know very well that Nath and I have been fighting untouchability tooth and nail, God knows since when, so that's not the issue. But your life has been patterned in a certain manner you have been brought up in a specific culture. To erase or to change all this overnight is just not possible. He is different in every way. You may not be able to handle it."

The major problem of the barrier between "the Savarna" and "Shudra" is thus presented. Saint Kabir, Saint Mira, Narsinh Mehta and Gandhiji tried their best to remove caste barriers, but it remains an age old problem. This problem has become complex because there has not been any realization of institutional religion in India. Tendulkar, in this play tries to show that vast gap exists between the life-style of the Savaran and the Shudra. So though, in the independent India the Dalit takes higher education, the psyche has not been changed and none of the two is able to accept the other. It is presented through the characters of Arun and Jyoti. Jyoti, like her father lives in a fantasy world and inspired by her father's Gandhian principle she wants to bring reformation. Nath believes that "Charity begins at home" and support his daughter in her decision of getting married to a dalit. The father and daughter want to provide "Space" to one dalit and dream about utopian society. But they are disillusioned at the end in their search for casteless or classless society and Tendulkar by presenting their disillusionment proves that the talk of "abolishing caste system or Varna system is useless.

This very urge of Tendulkar arouses the feeling that "Kanyadaan" is anti dalit play. But in order to present the psyche of dalit's mind the negative delineation of Arun's character is necessary. Tendulkar does not want to show the exploitation of untouchable of pre Independent India but, the plight of dalits in post independence India where abuse, physical torture, and dependence, are not showered but in the independent India ample opportunities are given to Dalits – education, job, economic independence, acceptance in the society, representation in politics and in religion. But for thousands of years they have been oppressed inhumanly so their psyche is not ready to accept "co-existence" with savaran. Though opportunities are provided they have accepted that they are "shudra" and "the saravan" cannot be their well wishers. It is just their hypocrisy and so Arun's behaviour in this respect does not shock us at all.

Arun is dalit, who is doing B.A and also working in "sramik samachar." Jyoti meets him in the socialists' study group. His parents are living in a village known as Chiroli. The family has seven children and Arun is second child of his parents, since his father does not earn enough from the farm, Arun has to work and he sends money home every month. Jyoti is familiar with him for the last two months only. She is impressed by his poems as he writes excellent poem. He is gifted with poetic mind. Though he is dalit, Goddess Sarswati has endowed him with poetic genius as God does not make difference in imparting knowledge to human beings. His poetic gift inspires him to write his autobiography and this poetic genius of Arun attracts Jyoti. As Jyoti says

"His poems and his autobiography have inspired me with complete faith in him."

Jyoti herself says that she has not fallen in love with Arun as she says

Arun said, you don't think that I am an absolutely worthless fellow I said not He said, this is incredible, and added in that case let us get married. And I nodded".

So, the idealistic upbringing and being the daughter of socialist she believes the idea, of getting married to a dalit is reformative as she finds good qualities in Arun. The mother Seva and brother Jayprakash oppose the very idea and it is decided they should invite Arun for a cup of tea to become acquainted with him.

**Nutan Gosavi** writes in **"Kanyadaan : An expose of political progressirves"**

"When Jyoti declares her intention to marry a Dalit boy, the parents are rattled but they are too seasoned as politicians to show their inner unease. They realize that now their integrity as public advocates of inter-caste marriages and casteless society is on test. Naturally, the parents reaction is cagey and guarded. Seva's response to the news displays a gap between her theory and practice. She finds one excuse after another to stop the marriage although she is self-rightous enough to say that she is not opposed to inter caste marriage per se. At first, she says that Jyoti is acting in haste and then she talks of the incompatibility of their lifestyle. In comparison, Nath's reaction is less ruffled and more in keeping with their professed ideology. But, the trouble here is that the more in accord with their public pronouncements, the more naive it appears."

The entry of Arun in Act I, scene II and the interview itself points out the life style of dalit and the psyche of a dalit boy. Each dialogue of Arun is enough to present the vast gap between the "Savaran and sudhra" Constantly he compares his life and Jyoti's life manner and life style. He does not even hesitate to satirize the "Savaran". He feels uncomfortable in the big house of Jyoti, which is not that much big but a house of higher middle class, But as a Dalit he lives in the last corner of the village, generally alone from the rest, Arun, says-

"If you see my father's hut you'll understand. Ten of us, big and small, lived in that eight feet by ten feet. The heat of our bodies warm us in winter no clothes on our back, no food in our stomach, but we felt very safe. Here these damn houses of the city people, they're like the bellies of sharks and crocodiles each one alone in them!

So, the residential matter is presented. The house is small but big enough to provide warmness & affection to ten people in comparison with the isolated life of the people who live in the big bunglows. Arun compares them with sharks and crocodiles. He feels suffocated in the four walls of cements and longs to merge into the crowd which provides him warmth.

During his visit to Jyoti's house Arun makes her aware about the life of Dalit. Critics find that Jyoti has sacrificed her life for the scavenger like Arun. But Arun is not at fault. He is not a deceiver but very frankly describes the life of dalit and warns Jyoti that her romantic world is totally different from the real world. She will not be able to adjust in the scavenger's world which evokes only, disgust to the civilized men. Arun's description of his life – the life of Dalit focus the plight of Dalits.

Arun says-

"Our grand fathers and great grand fathers used to roam, barefoot, miles and miles in the heat, in the rain, day and night.... Till the rags on their butt fell apart... used to wander shouting Johaar, Maayi- baap sir, Madam, sweeper'! and their calls polluted the Brahmins' ears."

With this very dialogue Tendulkar brings in to the drama the age old gap between the Shudras and Brahmins. In the 'Bhagavad Gita' we find a reference to divisions of caste according to quality and wok !

*caturvarnyam maya srstam gunakarmavibhagasah*

*tasya kartaram api mam viddly akartaram aviya yam.*

(The fourfoldorder was created by Me according to the divisions of quality and work. Though I am its creater know Me to be incapable of action of change.)

The emphasis here is on Guna - "aptitude' and karma "function" and not Jati - birth Dr. Radhakrishanan also expresses an opinion that fourfold order was designed for human evolution. There is nothing about the caste system, which has changed its character in the process of history. The present morbid condition of India broken into castes and subcastes is opposed to the unity taught by the Gita which stand for an organic as against an atomistic conception of the society.

The social difference in the Hindu society took the form of cast system. Caste system is not merely a division of labourers — which is quite different from division of labour — it is hierarchy in which the divisions of labourers are graded one above the othe [Dr. Babasaheb Amedkar : Writing and Speeches. Bombay Govt. of Maharastra, (1987) 67]

And dalit started the plightful journey of life. Even the traveller from China, Fahiyan (405 to 411) mentioned that "chandal has to live away from the village and when they enter they have to declare their entry before coming to the village". That was "Gupt Age" So in India 600 B.C., the untouchability was already prevalent. And still in 2008 it is still prevalent in the society. Arun further describes the miserable life of the Dalit He says –

"Generation after generation, their stomachs were used to the stale, stinking bread they have begged! Our tongues always tasting the flesh of dead animals, and with relish! Surely we can't fit into your unwrinkled Tinopal world. How can there be any give and take between our ways and your fragrant ghee spread, wheat bread culture?"

Arun truly gives the description of the life – style of Dalits. Their destiny is to eat, the left out eatables of others which also they begged. Even the flesh of dead animal becomes delicacy for them, such a life style is totally opposite to the civilized culture of the Savarans. Arun knows that Jyoti is brought up in a highly sophicated culture and she has only heard about the hardships and disgustful world of Dalit. But the practical life with Arun in which begging, abuse, beating, stinking food will prove to be hell for Jyoti. He asks therefore –

"Will you marry me and eat stinking bread with spoilt dal in my father's hut? Without vomiting? Tell me Jyoti, can you shit everyday in our slum's village toilet like my mother, Can you beg, quaking at every door, for a little grass for our buffaloes. Come on, tell me!

"You thought of marrying me. Our life is not the socialists service camp. It is hell and I mean hell. A hell named life."

This speech of Arun resembles with the famous poem of **Heera Dom**, written in **Bhojpuri** language. Which is titled as "**Achut ki shikayat**" and published in **1914 i**n the magazine "**Swarswati**." This poem is regarded as the first Dalit poem by dalit poet. In the forty lines of this poem the poet presents the condition and miseries of dalit along with religion government and people as well as the god.

They are pained by the abuse, and rude behaviour of savarns yet

the god does not grant happiness to them and no one even protests. Not only that but considering them as Dom" "Scavenger" people disgusted them. The poet says we work from dawn to dusk and get two rupees in the month.

We earn money by labour. The Thakur sleeps soundly at home and we work in the field. But who listens –

With anguish the poet says we drink water with the help of our palm. People do not allow us to be near to them and beat us with their shoes and we bow down and return their shoes with gratitude. The poet asks why do people hate them like these? Why are they regarded so mean and degrading?

So, even today this untouchability prevails in the society though law and order are there in the society. In the deaf and dumb society, it is difficult to give voice to alive community of "Dalit". It is voiced through poems from saint Raidas to Heera dome and the same anguish is presented by Tendulkar in this play through the character of Arun.

Arun wants to bring revolution. He wants to set the fire of revolt in which all the old customs, discriminations regarding caste, & class will be removed. Being aggressive and young he wants to kill upper class people He says. –

"At times a fire blazes - I want to set fire to the whole words, strangle throats, rape and kill. Drink up the blood of the beasts, your high caste society. I hen I calm down like the taantric when he comes out of his trance. Like a corpse, I live on.

So the fire of revolt burns within but limitations are given as he says just like corpse he is living physically. He is existing but all his sensitivity is dead seeing the injustice in the society. The fire extinguishes as economic, social, religious bondages are there.

Arun's anguish reminds the poem by Drarika Bharti, titled as " Sailab".

So "Hatred" or "Disgust" is inborn quality in Dalit as they face the injustice in the society and Arun is no exception. Arun realizes that he is causing Jyoti great pain by his outburst and he apologises to her asking her to forgive his mood for they arise out of his feeling of injustice, frustration, inner desire for revenge and his utter helplessness. It pleases Jyoti and she smiles. Arun in his excitement chants the childish rhyme. "Hasli re hasli, ek bamanee fasli."

Incidentally, the English translation in the text is a jolly game! Caught a Brahmin dame - does not bring out the full import of the Marathi rhyme. Besides very awkward. For non - Marathi readers it will be easier to grasp the meaning if it is translated as "see, she has smiled and therein is a Brahmin wench trapped." The word "Bamaneen" for a Brahmin woman is seen as uncouth and derogatory among Brahmins whereas, it is common for non-Brahmins to use the word "Shudra" or "Mharda " which is seen as casteist by the Dalit until recently freely used by nondalits. The first meeting of Arun with Jyoti's mother and brother is not at all positive. From the beginning Jyoti's mother is against this marriage so when they meet the caste prejudice is already there and when Arun gives the answer roughly, Seva, Jyoti's mother is shocked. Arun has also hidden hatred for the people of upper class. When Seva makes him aware about the hardships of city life and expenditures of city life as Arun has completed only B.A and not earning much, it would be difficult for him to provide luxury to Jyoti who is totally brought up in comfortable atmosphere. Arun thinks that Seva is mocking at his low status by reminding the expenditures of city life. In angry mood he gives the solution by saying.

"No problem. We shall be brewing illicit liquor. It is a first class profession for two persons. The man bribes the police and the wife serves customers. People call her aunty. The more striking the aunty's looks, the brisker the trade."

Seva is shocked by Arun's answer. Jyoti tries to make the atmosphere light but Arun who is already disturbed scolds her "you don't know a shit shut up". The father Mr. Nath arrives and being socialist, he is overjoyed finding Arun at home. He is happy at the thought that at last his home has become Indian in the real sense as they have broken the caste barrier. He warmly greets Arun and offers tea and snacks to him. After his departure Seva and Jayprakash reject him as Jyoti's suitor. They find him uncultured, uncivilized, and his misbehaviour to Jyoti, shock them. Seva says

"But I will never accept him as my Jyoti's husband. Never."

Jyoti is also confused and cannot give her frank opinion she says- At time I feel I can trust him, but the very next instant I am left miles behind him. I ask myself- this thing that I want to do, is it the right thing...? He is complex.

But Mr. Nath tries to convince them that he has been brought up in the midst of poverty and hatred. His psychological makeup is altogether different and they should try to understand him. He says in his favour – "He may not be a gentleman, but neither is he a scoundrel... He is like unrefined gold, he needs to be melted and moulded."

Mr. Nath, being Gandhian supports Jyoti's decision but Seva firmly objects and says-

"You ran your democracy. To me Jyoti's decision seems to be absolutely senseless and as her mother I cannot accept it... This is a home, not your, party, where you can impose your discipline." But Jyoti takes a revolutionary step and gets married to a dalit youth. By presenting this marriage Tendulkar does want to show the reformation of independent India but the play is a study of the psyche of Dalit. Reformation is not possible as they are not ready to leave their deep rooted life style. Any attempt by the upper class to uplift them is seen by them as a treachery, or merely a hypocrisy. So they do not accept the upliftment genuinely. It's difficult for them to imagine their lives without drink, abuse and beating and quarrels. Tendulkar does not want to show that a dalit youth has become a member of Brahmin family and lived happily but presents totally unexpected situation, as if Tendulkar tried to present the defeat of Gandhian ideal in the midst of Dalit world.

The married life of Jyoti and Arun is presented in dark light. An opportunity is given to a dalit boy to rise up in the society but Arun is shown incapable of utilizing that chance. He cannot escape from his Dalit mentality, and life style. Though educated, his wife Jyoti has become a mere thing for him on whom he can show his love whenever he is pleased and can show his anger by beating her if he is angry. Jyoti after months returns home and declares that she has left Arun forever. She says "He….. he will not enter this house. Because I have left him…. I am not going back to him again… never." I must tell you, Bhai. I must. I am fed up with him Fed up! Fed up!"

The mother, Seva feels relieved as Jyoti is released from the animal like Arun. But Arun, arrives to take Jyoti back home. Still he is not changed. Mr. Nath invites him for dinner but he says No, I am not fit to have dinner with people like you."

When Seva asks him the reason of the quarrel, he shocks them by saying that he has beaten Jyoti. He does not feel shy for his behaviour but defends himself by saying that abuse and beating are knitted in the webs of their lives. Jyoti is not used to such things so such things appear to her unnatural but it is part and parcel of their lives. He says –

"When have I claimed that I am civilized and cultured like your people, From childhood I have seen my father come home drunk everyday, and beat my mother half dead, see her cry her heart out. Even now I hear the echoes of her broken sobs. No one was there to wipe the tears."

For his behaviour he considers his upbringing as the key factor. The family life which he has seen consists of only abuses, beating and quarrels .Hence for him married life means love plus beating. His mother has tolerated such a life without complaint so it never occurs to him that a woman does not like it. Therefore Jyoti's behaviour to leave him sounds unfair to him. He says –

"What am I but the son of scavengers. We don't know the non violent ways of Brahmins like you. We drink and beat our wives….. we make love to them…. But the beating is what gets publicized."

For him the beating of the wife does not mean that he hates her. He loves her too, but according to him it is never appreciated but they are evaluated by their negative sides only. So he says "I am a barbarian, a barbarian by birth when have I claimed any white collar culture."

He does not even want to change himself because he does not want to lose his identity of Dalit. He believes that the upper class people only make a show of love for their wives but actually they never give "space" to them. After all it is a matter of being "Male" which is superior and "Wife" is merely a "second sex." Whether a male belongs to lower class or upper class, he dominates. He says.-

"I am what I am… and shall remain exactly that. And your Jyoti knew what I was even before she married me. In spite of that she married me, she did it out of her own free will."

And at last Jyoti decides to go with him despite the unwillingess of her mother and brother. Few months later in Act II, scene II it is presented that Jyoti is expecting a baby, and her mother admits her at the nursing home in the sixth month due to internal bleeding. Through the neighbour Seva comes to know that

Arun beats and kicks Jyoti at night. Mr. Nath is totally broken and finds it incredible as to how a man can beat a pregnant wife. Arun has recently written autobiographical novel which is sentimental as well as poetical. Mr. Nath, after reading it, is overjoyed and praised it like anything and now the disclosure of Jyoti's condition moves him and he laments —

"Such heinous behaviour by someone who wrote this beautiful autobiography? How can he? Here in these pages he describe the humiliations he has undergone with extraordinary sensitivity... and the same man kicks his pregnant wife on her belly? How...

Seva, who is already against the marriage, ironically comments that their dalit son- in- law, who writes lovely poems and wonderful autobiography, is an idler, who lives on the money of Jyoti and drinks and beats his wife. She sarcastically points out the reality which Tendulkar wants to convey in order to justify Arun's behaviour towards his wife. Seva says –

"Doesn't his wife belong to the high caste? In this way he is returning all the kicks aimed at generations of his ancestors by men of high caste. It appears that this is the monumental mission he has set out to fulfill."

And here, Seva is absolutely right. Tendulkar does not want to present Arun with negative shades but he explores the psyche of a Dalit youth. Arun loves Jyoti very much but the Dalit part of his mind lives in his tormented past and unleashes torment on his high-caste wife. His past returns to haunt him every night and he turns into unpredictable savage beast, who has strange malice and, a sadistic desire to punish his wife for the suffering his ancestors have gone through the ages. He has crude satisfaction that he has "Caught a Brahmin dame." Not only the daughter is punished but Arun derives sadistic pleasure in abusing her parents too. Seva who is the leader of Sevadal is accused by Arun as a procuress who supplies girls from the Sevadal to the socialist leaders. Arun even accuses that Jyoti's real father is not Mr. Nath but "Guruji", the guide, and philosopher of Seva. Thus, by such accusation Arun tries to degrade morally the parents of Jyoti and thereby takes revenge on the upper caste. Arun's autobiographical novel gets published and he has become a celebrated Dalit writer. The association known as "The Progressive Dalit Literature Circle" has arranged a discussion on his autobiography. Arun along with other members, like Hammeer Rao Kamle, essayist of dalit literature, Vamanseth Nevrgaonkar, critic of dalit literature, arrives to invite Mr.Nath to preside over the function of the discussion on his autobiography as Mr. Nath is a socialist, an MLA and also his father-in - law. Mr. Nath does not want to take part in the discussion and to appreciate the book. Arun, the writer merely a hypocrite like a savage beast is antagonist of the upper caste. He does not miss this situation. He reminds Mr. Nath about the social criticism if he was not present in the function. People would conclude that father in law and son-in-law are not in a good terms. The rise of the son-in-law could not be endured by the fathers-in-law etc. He further tries to convince him by reminding the gap between the upper caste and lower caste. Mr. Nath's rejection may be due to the fact that he does not want to mix with lower class people. Arun says –

"Your connections are with the elite. Our friends here belong to a low caste, brought up on the flesh of dead animals. Our ancestors trudged around with a load of shit on their heads. It is my great good fortune which made a fair and lovely bird from a well to do, high class background fall to my lot. My revered mother in law has always been angry with me. She would have liked a fair, rich, highly educated son in law with his butt glued to a high office chair. But fate wrote my name instead. A poet and a writer! And dalit at that!"

Again Arun's mind remembers the miserable plight of his ancestors who trudged in the realm of shit only and passed away. They never came above or their voice remained unheard only due to higher caste people who exploited them. This reality haunted Arun's mind and its memory he carries wherever he goes. The slightest rejection, or neglect is enough to remind him the fact that he belongs to "low caste" and so "rejection is his destiny. He is of the view that Mr. Nath is hypocrite as in the society Mr. Nath stands for liberal socialist ideas who has done many social works for the downtrodden, but actually he hates them from within, he does not like a dalit son in law so in this evocative scene

Arun ridicules Nath by saying –

"These people believed you were a well wisher of the dalit community. That you championed the cause of "a well in every village for the dalit" you launched a satyagrah for that cause. You deliver socialist addresses at the state Assembly. With the trumpet call of idealism you got your daughter married to a dalit. This taunting of Arun breaks Mr. Nath totally. Now he really starts hating him. May be Mr. Nath's two-facedness comes out when he is "offended" by the Dalit contemptuous mockery of him and after Arun's departure he says –

"His visit has polluted this drawing room, this house and this day… It stinks Seva you know you see I feel like taking a bath like cleaning myself, clean everything ! This furniture, this floor… all this … he has made them filthy, dirty, polluted!"

Inspite of his unwillingness, for the sake of his daughter, so that Arun can not torement Jyoti more, he goes to the function. He praises the book publicly but Jyoti condemns her father as she knows that the speech of Mr. Nath was fake. Inwardly he hates Arun. Even Jyoti is disillusioned in her search of reformation. She suffers due to the idealism taught by her father. For Arun she is only a daughter of "savarna" who can never be his wife and the play ends when she takes up another mission to be the wife of a dalit and she leaves the house of her parents by saying that she is Jyoti Arun Athavale, a scavenger, because she has realized that only when she will live with dalit – live like insect only then the distance between the "savarna" and "shudra" can be crossed.

So the play explores the issue of Dalit's psyche in the post independent India. They are not ready to mingle with the main stream of the society. They want to maintain their Identity of Dalit.

The genuine concern of the higher class people appears to them merely hypocrisy as they can not forget their intolerable past. The suppression of them in the past by the "savarna" haunts them and this reality is presented through Arun's character. Tendulkar wants to suggest that if this is the reality how can the gap between the savarna and shudra be bridged? The idealism of few people to mingle with them will never work so the situation demands new means to overcome the gap between the upper class and lower class.

In order to present this reality Tendulkar has to depict the character of Arun with negative shades. So the play raises anti-dalit feelings. When the writer Meghna Pethe told Tendulkar that Dalit writers were angry about his misrepresentation of Dalits, the playwright observed testily.

"I pointed a gun at a wholly different target. What can I do if something else falls dead."

So "Kanyadaan" had fired at its salvos not at Dalits, against the hypocrisy of secular liberals, "People of my generation" who refused to face realities, and adopted easy solutions for complicated issues. Such illusions were bound to end in disaster.

# 4. GANDHIAN IDEALISM
# VERSUS
# THE REALITY

Kanyadaan remains revelant even after 26 years. Tendulkar does not explore the issue of Dalit's psyche but also presents the vainness of Gandhian principles in Indian social structure, Karl Marx through his theory of "Dialectical materialism" talked about the abolishment of the lower, class and upper class. In India, the great man Gandhiji along with the talk of non violence and truth tried to remove 'untouchability' from the Indian society. It affected few people of India, who wanted to build new India on the principles of Gandhiji. But the post independent Indian society and its people are still not ready to follow the Gandhian principles in establishing new social structure. They have their own problems and views and so they are unable to mingle with the new social structure imagined by the idealist.

The play explores serious issues of caste divide, co existence and idealism in an atmosphere wreathed in strain and strife Mr. Nath Devlalikar, is a socialist, Gandhian, democrat MLA. who has practiced Gandhian principles in his home also and feeds his two children Jyoti and Jayprakash on his idealism. The play is not about the glorification of Gandhian idealism but in this play Tendulkar depicts the disillusionment of Mr. Nath regarding the Gandhian principles. He is a political visionary and wants to create an utopian world on the base of Gandhian idealism but the end of the play presents that his idealism crumbles and he accepts the reality that social change in Indian society is impossible. For his realization he sacrifices his daughter.

From Act I, his disillusionment regarding the working of the nation is depicted. The play presents post independence era of India. Whatever hardships, struggle India did, the fruit was, gained in the form of "Freedom" and the Gandhians hoped for liberal, democratic honest, government But it proves to be merely a "vision". Mr. Nath wants an inquiry regarding the departing time of the bus for Asangaon But the controller fails to give him any information and Mr. Nath laments that such irresponsibility will never develop the independent nation. The controller must be fully informed about every single bus which departs from his terminal as he is appointed for that purpose only. He laments "The visions we had of the future of this nation before Independence! And what we are forced to see today! Disgusting. It hurts!"

So, he knows that independent India is going astray and Gandhian principles remain in the books. But he is contented as he practices the principles in his personal life and does not merely teach it. He is not an orthodox father who dominates the lives of the children but practices democracy at home also. He has taught his children his idealism unaware about its destructive effect. When his daughter Jyoti wants to talk about her affair he says.

"Tell me something say it then. Who stops you? We have a democracy in this house and we are proud of it. Democracy outside and dictatorship in the home, we don't know these two timing tricks.

He wholeheartedly welcomes Jyoti's idea of getting married to a Dalit. He feels proud that his children, like him too follow the Gandhian principle and tries to reform the society. The progressive views of Mr. Nath inspire his daughter who wants to marry a Dalit and promises in delivering him from his devilish tendencies. Her father's lofty ideals have inculcated in her a spirit which tries to find the good in people, and strive to transform them. Mr. Nath gets excited and congrates his daughter for her idea. He is the only person who favours the daughter against the dislike of her mother. He rejects every argument of his wife Seva, who is also socialist. Mr. Nath, is optimist and hopes that Jyoti's decision will certainly enlighten the dark life of a dalit. He says –

If they decide to do so, lifestyles can certainly be changed. And the ideal of stability can be different for every man......

Even during his first meeting with Arun, he makes the atmosphere very light and comfortable by offering tea to him. He is true Gandhian and against drinking. He belongs to upper middle class where drinking is considered to be status but as he says

"Arun, Let us celebrate over a cup of tea. Well, nowadays our socialists don't mind even liquor. But in this matter I continue to be somewhat old fashioned. A little worm called Gandhi ate into my brain in youth didn't he, therefore certain things slipped out of my life forever. Liquor is one, fancy clothes is another…

It is not a matter of pride for him that he does not drink but genuinely he keeps away from this bad habit. But it is his sad destiny that he gets a son in law who is a drunkard and talks of brewing illicit liquor. So Mr. Nath's Gandhian world is put in conflict with the world of reality, where only vices prevail. Like "Dry Day" he is against "Untouchability". Just as Gandhiji has given the name "Harijan" to all "shudra' and place them near to God by calling them "Harijan", Mr. Nath, being Brahmin, does not feel hatred for them. Arun, appears to him as the proper suitor for his daughter. He says, "Seva, until today." 'Break the caste system' was a mere slogan for us I've attended many intercaste marriages and made speeches. But today I have broken the caste barrier in the real sense. My home has become Indian in the real sense of the term."

The matter of marrying a dalit invites firey argument in the family and the wife Seva strongly opposes it on the ground of culture and life style But Mr. Nath defends Arun.

"Manners and culture, are they your ancestral property? He is a good boy... he is well behaved... can anyone be that without culture?"

He feels surprised that his ideology is not understood by his wife, then what about the world? He strongly believes in Gandhiji's ideology to mingle the downtrodden with the main stream.Only then the barrier between the lower class and upper class can be crossed. Opportunity should be given and his family is taking the leadership. He convinces his wife.

"Look Seva, society cannot be transformed through words alone we have to act as catalysts in this transformation. The old social reformers did not stop with making speeches and writing articles on widow remarriage. Many of them actually married widows, why did they do it...? That was also an experiment, a difficult experiment, but they dared to risk it."

So, he becomes the practitioner of his preaching and establishes "charity begins at home". He has hope that this bold step of his daughter would not merely cross the barrier but it would set an example for other upper caste members to follow. He is of the opinion that Jyoti's journey of reformation will enlighten others and in future the nation will be without any casteism.

But he gets disillusionment regarding his ideology. The married life of Jyoti and Arun proves futile. Mr. Nath's idealism, breaks into pieces after the marriage of Jyoti and Arun. Jyoti soon realizes that Arun is not the man whose poetry she adored, he is a Dalit, whose past returns to haunt him every night and he unleashes torment on his high caste wife. He is a beast one moment, a lover the next, the devil and the poet are one and the same person, they cannot be separated, neither can he be cleansed of the vices like drinking, wife beating, which are a part of him. She leaves him and comes to her father for shelter Mr. Nath who believes in goodness in everyone is not ready to accept the reality. Gandhian principle cannot be vain, Jyoti has taken the right decision according to him. She should not leave Arun as it will take time for her to get adjusted herself in the world of Dalit. For him Arun is still good and his idealism will certainly work out, it may not remain in the book. He says

"Seva, let not this wonderful experiment fail! This dream which is struggling to turn real, let it not crumble into dust before our eyes! We will have to do something. We must save this marriage. Not necessarily for our Jyoti's sake... This is not just a question of our daughter's life, Seva this has.... A far wider significance .... This experiment is a very precious experiment."

So, he is a man, who has faith in the process of reformation. He wants Jyoti should set an example in the society that casteism is not barrier between two souls, but "LOVE" governs the world. When Arun arrives to take Jyoti back home he is overjoyed. The lamentation of Arun makes him understand that he is regretting and his experiment will be successful when Jyoti decides to go, he permits and says -

"Jyoti, I feel so proud of you, The training I gave you has not been in vain."

Arun writes auto-biography and Mr. Nath praises it wholeheartedly. He feels proud that Jyoti has selected such a man who moves the heart of everyone with his writing. But the revelation by his wife that Jyoti who is preganant, is in the hospital due to the kicking of Arun, Mr. Nath is shocked. His ideal world is shattered. His experiment has failed. He realizes that modern world cannot be run by "Bapu's" ideology. The sacrifice of his daughter's life has gone in vain. Arun remains the same and proves that the barrier between lower caste and upper caste cannot be crossed. Arun invites him for the discussion on his autobiography organized by the Progressive Dalit Literature Circle. Mr. Nath is not ready to attend the function and praise the person and the book, because Arun, even as a human being not as a Dalit appears to him disgusting, who writes with sensitivity on the humiliations of Dalit and the same man kicks the pregnant wife. He is not ready to praise such a hypocrite, Arun excites him to accept the invitation by reminding the social criticism but he is firm and says "NO" to Arun. Now he is totally disillusioned. Instead of appreciation for Dalit, he has disgust and hatred for them. At the cost of his only daughter he made out the experiment but it proves futile. Now he realizes that Gandhian principle to remove untouchability, is impossible as Dalit themselves are not ready to mix with the upper caste. The miserable past has gone deep into the psyche of the Dalit and the members of the upper caste are just only a tool for them to take revenge. He remembers his son Jayprakash's words and agrees.

"In other words, yesterday's victim is today's victimizer. If he has been, shot at yesterday, he shoots today……"

He feels insulted as his mild, soft nature is taken by Arun as a sign of powerlessness but now he proves to be the angry father of Jyoti and decides that he will never deliver a speech for Arun but Seva, his wife reminds him that his decision may be true but his refusal will bring more suffering for Jyoti, Arun will take revenge on Jyoti, and Jyoti is pregnant. Mr. Nath's refusal will make Arun to find new ways to torment her. She says

"If you don't go to the meeting, God knows what he….. in his madness.. will do to Jyoti…. Therefore, you will have to go, you will have to praise the book, because that is the only option left to us."

Here, Mr. Nath finds himself powerless before the predicament of his daughter, and praises his son in law's autobiography in the function, applause showering from his mouth and passion dripping from his eyes. He hopes that,

"My blatant lying today will make Jyoti's life a little more tolerable. I did it for the sake of my brave and innocent daughter. What is this compared to her having ruined her whole life for my sake?"

So, he makes a glowing speech, showering accolades on the book. All this he had to do to preserve his progressive image in the public and also to ensure that it spares his daughter from getting beaten. For the first time perhaps he has said what he did not feel at heart. He breaks down completely by the painful awareness of his utter helplessness in the matter which forces him to carry this hypocritical task so repugnant to him.

The father who has taught his daughter the lofty ideals of humanity and socialism is defeated. He finds that his hope in human innocence is faulty and how she is a victim of his faith in pursuing this promise.

He says –

"I had this maniacal urge to uproot casteism and caste distinctions from our society. As a result, I pushed my own daughter into a sea of misery……"

This is self-knowledge indeed!

Being Gandhian he never speaks lie in the public but in the function he praised the autobiography which is not based on the truth. And in order to praise the book he had used the most beautiful world and writer like Byron and Kusumargraj only for the sake of his daughter. So that Arun can keep her happy. He thinks "what is her fault? Why does she suffer?" The only crime she has committed is that she had taken her father's words for gospel truth. She adopted her father's values and was guided by her father's humanism and liberalism. He hopes that his daughter will be happy as he has praised Arun in public.

But in the last scene of the play the exchange of words between father and daughter is surprising. Jyoti confronts her father's charitable, gesture in releasing his son-in-law's autobiography. Throughout her life she has observed her father frank and honest and today due to Arun he also became hypocrite and praised the book against his will. She says –

"Your speech today was not only lousy, it was a hireling's speech. You attended the meeting against your wishes you praised that book against your wishes."

She does not like this charitable act of her father who still considers her to be the member of Brahmin's family. She boldly says she now belongs to different family. She says –

"I belong to someone who makes your clean and pure soul impure by his touch."

Jyoti makes the father realize that all his teaching has gone in vain. Her father has always told her that no man is fundamentally evil, he is good, he has certain propensities towards evil. They must be transformed and the earth will become heaven. It is essential to awaken the God slumbering within man. But through her own experience she has learnt that this idealism is totally false. She says –

"Putting man's beastliness to sleep and awakening the godhead within is an absurd notion. You made me waste twenty years of my life before I could discover this."

In a fit of anger, she denounces the teaching of her father and says –

"Come and watch Arun at night when he staggers home roaring drunk, if you have the guts. There is a savage beast in his eyes, his lips, his face…. In every single limb. And bestiality is something which cannot be separated from him. In the beginning like an idiot, I used to search for that Arun who is above and beyond this beastliness. I used to call out to him, take him in my arms. Hard experience taught me I would always fail. Arun is both the beast and the lover. Arun is the demon and also the poet. Both are bound together one within the other, they are one."

Mr. Nath tries to convince her and proposes that if she wants to reject him he is ready to support her. But Jyoti tells that he has taught them that one must not turn one's back upon the battlefield. It is cowardly to bow down to circumstances. She reminds her father that you taught us the poems which said

"I march with utter faith in the goal!"

"I grow with rising hopes"

"Cowards stay ashore, every wave opens a path for me."

And according to her, this drug has entered and mingled with her blood and it has numbed her entire consciousness. She cannot run away.She says, She will follow.

"March on, oh soldier! and continue to lose our lives as guinea pigs in the experiment."

Mr. Nath's experiment to reform the society has totally failed. His own daughter is blaming him for teaching the principle of goodness and humanity. Gandhian doctrine may shine glorious on the pages but in real life its practice is futile just as in the film "Lage Raho Munnabhai" it is shown, that modern India has forgotten Gandhi, though the "Bapu" lives in India through the names of road, pictures, statues, image on rupee, etc. but where he should live, in the "Heart" is totally missing. People do not understand or follow his principle of "Non-violence" or "Truth" and it sounds "Ridiculous" to most of the Indians. Plato, wants to establish an Ideal state where he will not allow poets or poetry as poetry is based on falsehood and it depicts the imaginary realities regarding gods and great heroes. The gods are presented as quarrelsome, envious, jealous, greedy and it may corrupt the younger minds so he will allow only hymns to his ideal state. He asks the governess to tell only those stories which have good moral in it. But it is argued that if a child gets only one-sided knowledge, if he is taught only the goodness, will he be able to cope up with the world in which he will have to live? The world is not good but full of vice and so he must be aware about it. In this manner, Mr. Nath has always taught only good lesson, faith in human being and under its effect the daughter has selected a Dalit to remove untouchability but her experiences has taught her different reality. She realizes that if she will live as a Dalit only then the distance will be crossed and her father's experiment will be successful. So she says –

"I am not Jyoti Yadunath Devlalikar now, I am Jyoti Arun Athavale, a scavenger. I don't say harijan. I despise the term. I am an untouchable, a scavenger. I am one of them. Don't touch me. Fly form my shadow, otherwise my fire will scorch your comfortable values.

These last words of the play as opined by Nutan Gosavi "neatly sum up Jyoti's reaction about Nath as her philosopher and guide and more painfully as her father. It is often said that in a marriage a father loses his daughter, but in Nath's case the Kanyadaan – giving away of the daughter – has been doubly painful in his giving away Jyoti to Arun. He has lost her in more ways than one. His kanyadaan has turned out to be a sacrifice of his daughter on the altar of his socio-political ideology.

Thus, through a multi-layered content, Tendulkar finally drives home the point that the reality of one man is different from what the other man perceives it to be. The daughter finds her own reality in a filthy slum, where her man returns roaring drunk every night to beat her up one moment and caress the next. And once she realizes she must love Arun, the man and not Arun, the poet, she finds peace but not without discovering the emptiness of her father's idealistic rhetoric.

# 5. DRAMATIC TECHNIQUES OF KANYADAAN

Tendulkar writes

"Theater is a visual medium as much as it is a medium of words. This visual aspect needs to be used properly not only to create a relief in the barrage of continuously emoted words, but also to provide powerful visual insights into the complex content of the play. A play staged in a theatre is not a radio-play to be heard with closed eyes and enjoyed. The visual elements in a stage play, if not used properly can work against the magic of words and harm the play."

Kanyadaan is a play with two acts and five scenes. It is naturalistic play. The interesting thing about the play is that though the play explores serious issues of caste divide, coexistence and idealism yet for its presentation variety of scenes are superbly omitted. It is the dramatic art of Tendulkar that the whole action of the drama is presented only in the drawing room. The play is set throughout in the drawing room of the Devlalikars adorned with typical high-caste urban antique furniture with a picture frame of Mahatma Gandhi, Achary a Narendra Dev, Yusuf Meherali and Sane Guruji hanging from the wall complete with a creeper to resemble the garden outside.

Family jokes are plentiful to suggest liberal views of the Brahmin family like –

"The call of the nation is far more important than the call of a wife"

When Seva, the mother declares –

"If he had been a democratic, would I have been his wife?"

Or the ability of Mr. Nath to make fun of himself.

"That's why I've lasted so long in politics" and

"One can take a first class nap during the dull speeches at the session."

So, the play is laced with a gentle humour which presents happy family of Mr. Nath Devalikar.

This gripping play, which is decorated with fine dashes of humour, is charged with an undercurrent of violence, uncertainities and anger but it is the art of Tendulkar that violence is not presented on the scene but only brilliantly reported. Arun is depicted as a drunkard who beats his wife frequently even during pregnancy and speaks abuses. Abuses and beating are not presented but reported through the speech of Seva and Jyoti and through the speech hatred for Arun is presented.

The play ends with Mr. Nath's whimper. Mr. Nath is disillusioned regarding his faith in Gandhian principle, humanity and Idealism. He is defeated as his experiment has failed though he sacrificed his daughter. In order to suggest this, the dramatist uses the sounds of huge buildings hurtling down. The crashing of buildings gets louder to suggest his despair. Mr. Nath breaks down. This final whimper appears as a heartrending purgatory wail which could make a person cry. The dramatist through this scene creates Catharsis, the feeling of pity and fear. The audience feels "Pity" for Mr. Nath's defeat in his search for ideal society. He does not deserve such an end, where the daughter confronts him and blames him. He is good and always taught goodness to his children, but the world is not ready to accept this. And his condition also arouses the feeling of "fear" and the spectators think that if they follow the same idealism, they have to suffer like Mr. Nath as the world is not run by ideal view but one should be practical. So Tendulkar, brings classical Hamartia at the end. A woman crying does not have so much impact because the audience expects it, but a man crying can just destroy mental peace and "Kanyadaan" becomes an amazing play, with amazing script.

# 6. CONCLUSION

None can deny the fact that literature of every time and space springs from the cultural ethos of that time and space. The natural accordance is always to be found between the literature of a particular time, space and society of that time and space. Literature springs from culture and hence with all its aesthetics it proves to be a social and cultural document of that particular time and space. The bond between literature and culture is an everlasting phenomenon. The basic reason why this tuning is to be found between literature and the cultural ethos is the commitment of the writer. Writer experiences a greater commitment to his time and space and writes with a vision of reality as well as responsibility. His aim is to see and sees the prevailing norms of his culture in a real sense of the term and so he becomes a committed person, a committed writer. His status as a writer would be futile if there is no sense of responsibility or tone of commitment in his works. The first thing that can be concluded on the basis of the present research work on Vijay Tendulkar's plays is that he is a playwright with a conscious sense of commitment. A writer who desires to be aesthetic in his approach of writing, should in no way give himself a consent to connive at the prevailing realities of his time, culture and society. Tendulkar remains faithful not only in observing those realities but also in displaying them through his plays. He is a dramatist with commitment to his time and country. His plays are adorned with aesthetic value but he does not try to escape from his commitment. It can be justified more elaborately on the basis of his plays.

As a playwright he holds a mirror through his works before the society which is very much Indian and the society finds its own reflection in that mirror. Nothing of Society – good and evil, high and low, black and white – remains, unseen or unnoticed to him. His plays present before the spectators both the sides of life of an average Indian.

Tendulkar as a playwright reflects both the sides of Indian life – the bright side as well as the dark one. As Gouri Ramanarayan aptly observes "with his exposure to Marathi theatre form childhood and journalistic background Vijay Tendulkar turned contemporary socio-political situation into explosive drama". He has dwelt on the alienation of the modern individual, satirized contemporary politics, forcefully depicted social and individual tensions, portrayed with finesse the complexities of human character and vigorously exploited man-woman relationship in several of his works. Significantly the themes which have engaged his most frequent attention, have been the plight of woman in a maledominated urban middle class society, and the husband-wife relationship as obtained in metropolitan centers like Bombay and Delhi. Vijay Tendulkar portrays the contemporary society and the predicament of man in it with a special focus on the morbidity in his plays. His plays touch almost every aspect of human life in the modern world and share the disillusionment of the post- modern intellectuals. However, he seems to highlight three major issues: gender, power and violence.

A close study of Vijay Tendulkar's plays reveals that Tendulkar is not a teacher or preacher. He is not one of those dramatists who use their medium in the service of their favourite socio-political ideology. He is not out to propagate any particular philosophy of life. Some critics have pointed out leftist interpretation to the plays like Ghashiram Kotwal, Kamala and Sakharam Binder. It shows that his plays are open to diverse interpretations and cannot be tied down to a single line of thinking. So the question whether Tendulkar writes for life's sake or art's sake is pointless. All that we can say is that he seems to favour socialist humanism but it should also be remembered that his plays do not revolve in the orbit of that ideology either.

It is significant to note most of Tendulkar's plays are gyno-centric. He was essentially dealing with a world, which in the guise of the modern ideal of nuclear family rejected woman's independence as a citizen, enforced traditional Hindu-Brahmin norms of behavior, crushed her attempts of gaining freedom and exercised a rigid control on her sexuality and productivity.

In Silence! Sakharam Binder and the Vultures, Tendulkar deals with the unconventional theme of sex and violence, but a shift in his concerns is evident when he professes emphatically that man is constantly and violently seeking after positions of power and he would work on this "basic theme" hereafter. In fact, he became aware of moral values in the modern political system. His dramatic creation reflects his concern for common man who, caught in the matrix of opportunistic ethics of modern world, feels alienated. **Ghashiram Kotwal** shows how a common man hero, seeking, power, confronts the people who are already in power and undergoes an organic change. Though, it is based on historical legend, is not actually a historical play. Unlike other dramatists Tendulkar finds a parallel running between antiquity and modernity. Ghashiram Kotwal tells the story of a person who, confronted with a world of hypocrisy and inhumanity, learns to play a careerist falling in line with prevailing ethics and becomes a martyr. The play gains in metaphoric dimension as the central character's obsession with power results in the loss of his identity. Ghashiram is transformed from an ordinary person to a tyrannical executor. The play also demonstrates how a historical event cast in folk theatre could be used to depict the evils perpetrated by a lecherous ruler who not only shuts his eyes to but also indirectly aggravates the material and moral decadence that has set in the society around him and who creates an avenging monster just to cover up his amorous life.

**Kanyadaan** is perhaps the most controversial of all the plays written by Tendulkar. It dwells on an extremely sensitive social and political issue, namely, the conflict between upper castes and Dalits, a phenomenon still prevalent in several parts of India. He raises disturbing questions, but never bothers to answer them. This method of his is truly characteristic of a genuine playwright whose foremost concern is to open his readeraudiences' eyes to a social problem which continues to evade easy solutions. It demonstrates how the ideal people, devoid of realistic vision, not only fail to achieve their cherished aim but also create new problems. Moreover, the children of these ideal people often become victims of their experiments with their ideals. Jyoti the central character of the play, accepts her father's ideal of casteless society and sincerely pursues it. In doing so, she risks her marital life. The play is branded as an anti-dalit play and there was much controversy about it. Here also the issue of gender relations emerges. Jyoti becomes a site, a battle ground on which the clash between the upper caste and the Dalit castes takes shape. She becomes the vessel in which the conflicting caste ideologies pour their aspirations for power. The complete submission of the girl's gendered self to the violence perpetrated on her by the caste politics leaves no scope for even an ideological alternative. That she deliberately chooses to become the model, ideal, Hindu, Brahmin housewife to him, that she will call her husband's people and home her own, sacrifice her career for him and mutely suffer all the physical, sexual and psychological violence and humiliation inflicted upon her by him is the problem of the play. The entire process of posing the problem here seems to raise interesting questions. Inter-caste marriage has been offered as a solution to the caste problem. But this resolution of the problem leads us to believe that finally the marriage institution is sacrosanct. Jyoti has to tread the path of self annihilation.

The analysis of Vijay Tendulkar's plays show that his commitment remains the same in each of his plays. His plays put forth burning issues of the contemporary society and times without allowing himself to interfere. He presents on the stage characters as free individuals who live according to their inner will and inner landscape that gives the touch of reality to his plays. Nowhere his characters sound as puppets in his hands. They live, love and suffer because of their own way of life. They are round and dynamic in nature, whether they remain for short or long span of time before the audience. Tendulkar believed that the playwright needs to be an actor-writer who plays 'roles' as he writes, and it helped Tendulkar in depicting the characters as he was associated with the theatre. According to him characterization in a play is to a large extent revealed through the dialogue. Therefore the playwright must have a mouldable and not a rigid style of writing. He must change his style with every character and Tendulkar as a playwright followed this.

Each of his characters reveal a new pattern of characterization. Sakharam represents the impotent fury of male masochism. Ramakant and Umakant present vulturine instinct of human beings'avarice, cunningness, lust, ruthlessness. Ghashiram represents lust for Power. Jaisingh Jadav's character is study of success-oriented modern man. Mr. Nath of "Kanyadaan" represents Ganadhian ideology. His women characters truly exemplify Santa Gokhale's remark that they are romanticized, idealized or forced to live by their creator's symbolic purposes. They are first and foremost human beings of flesh and blood who drew their features from the widest range of observed examples. They are allowed to inhabit the entire spectrum for the unbelievably gullible to the clever, from the malleable to the stubborn, from the conservative to the rebellious, from the self-sacrificing to the grasping. Leela Benare, Manik, Champa, Seva, are unconventional heroines, whereas Laxmi, Rama, Kamala, Sarita, Lalita Gauri, Jyoti, Mrs. Kashikar appear as victims in the patriarchal world.

"Theatre is a visual medium as much as it is a medium of words. This visual aspect needs to be used properly not only to create a relief in the barrage of continuously emoted words but also to provide powerful visual insights into the complex content of the play. A play staged in a theater is not a radio play to be heard with closed eyes and enjoyed. The visual element in a stage play, if not used properly can work against the magic of words and harm the play."

A play has a structure. Structure does not mean the plot or the story of the play. It is a framework. It is not visible but is felt." These views of Tendulkar enabled him to remain "experimental" in his plays. Even in commercial drama he made room for himself and had maintained his uniqueness. His plays reveal his art in maintaining economy of words, the ability to express maximum meaning in minimum words. His use of language is marked by an intelligent use of the punctuation marks, blank spaces, full stops and exclamation marks are effectively used by him. The play within the play technique in "Silence! The Court is in session" for the first time in Marathi drama opened up a new height of Drama. In "Kamala" the motif of the hectic phone calls, the device of the fading of lights, suggesting, in an oblique fashion are worth noting.

The success or failure of any work of art depends upon its appeal – whether that appeal proves to be transitory or everlasting. A work of art with an everlasting appeal always remains eternal. It will not be out of the way or excessive exaggeration if the same thing is said about Tendulkar's plays. We do notice even today victims like Kamala, Benare, Sarita, Rama, Lalita Guari in Society. At the same time we notice even today males likes Arun, Sakharam, Ramakant and Umakant, Jaisingh Jadav, Ghashiram etc. as long as such characters are there in our society, the appeal of his plays would remain intact. His plays will never lose the quality of relevance with which they have been written.

# BIBLIOGRAPHY

## PRIMARY SOURCES

- **Tendulkar, Vijay** – *Collected Plays in Translation,* (Oxford University Press, 2003.)

- **Tendulkar, Vijay** – *Ghashiram Kotwal,* Seagull Books, Calcutta,    2002

## SECONDARY SOURCES

- **Abrams M.H.** *"A Glossary of Literary Terms"* Macmillian. 1996

- **Abrams Teera**, *"Folk Theatre in Maharashtrian Social Development programme,"* Educational Theatre Journal 1975

- **Babu M.R.** *Political Deformity, In Indian drama Today,* Prestige -  Books – 1990

- **Babu M.S.** *"Spiritual Deformity,"* In Indian Drama Today, Prestige Books – 1990.

- **Babu, Sarat M.** *"Indian Drama Today",* New Delhi, Prestige Books, 1997

- **Banerjee Arundhati**, *Introduction Five plays by Vijay Tendulkar ,* Oxford up, Bombay

- **Bhalla M. M,** *"Folk Theatre and operas",* A Handful of Dreams Kantas Book Depot, 1977, Delhi.

- **Bhasin Kamala & Khan Nighat** Said *"Some questions on Feminism and its relevance in South Asia,"* ISBN New Delhi  - 1993.

- **Bhatnagar M.K.** *"Indian writings in English"* Atlantic publishers, New Delhi.

- **Bhatnagar M.K.,** *Feminist English Literature,* Atlantic Publishers New Delhi

- **Bhave Pushpa** *"Vijay Tendulkar : A Study in Contemporary Indian Theatre",* Sangit Natak Akademi, New Delhi – 1989.

- **Bhayani Utpal** – *સામાજિક નાટક, એક નૂતન ઉન્મેષઃ વિજય તેંડુલકર,* NavBharat Sahitya Mandir 1993.

- **Das Bijay Kumar** – *Critical Essay on post-colonial literature,* Atlantic Publishers.- 2001

- **Das Bijay kumar.** *"Comparative Literature,"* Atlantic Publishers, New Delhi.

- **Deshpande G.P** *"Modern Indian Drama,"* An Anthology, Sahitya Akademi, New Delhi  2002

- **Dharan N.S.** *"The plays of Vijay Tendulkar"* Creative Books – New Delhi – 1999

- **Dharan N.S.** *"The Plays of Vijay Tendulkar",* Creative Books, 1999

- **Dhawan R.K.** *"20 years of Indian writing",* IAES, New Delhi 1999.

- **Dodiya J.K. & Surendran K.V.** *"Indian English Drama, Critical Perspectives,"* Sarup & Sons – 2002

- **Gargi, Balwant.** *Theatre in India,* New York: Theatre Arts, 1962.

- **Gayle Greene and Coppelia Kahn**, *"Feminist scholarship and the Social construction of woman,"* Making a Difference : Feminist Literary criticism, London, Methuen – 1985.

- **George, K.M., ed.** *Comparative Indian Literature,* Madras: Macmillan, 1984.

- **Gowda, Anniah.** *Indian Drama,* Mysore: Univ. of Mysore, 1974.

- વણકર ભી. ન – અનુસંધાન, ગુર્જર એજન્સી, ગાંધીમાર્ગ, અમદાવાદ.

- વણકર ભી.ન. – નવોન્મેષ, ભગવતી ઓફસેટ , અમદાવાદ

- વણકર ભી. ન. – દલિત સાહિત્ય, પૂનમ ઓફસેટ, ગાંધીનગર

- **Jyenger, K.R.S.**, *Indian writing in English,* Sterling publishers – 1985. New Delhi

- **Karnad Girish** *"Author's Introduction,"* Three Plays, Oxford University press, Delhi, 1994.

- **Karnad Girish** *"Nag Mandal"* & *"Hayavadana,"* Oup – 1993.

- **Kumar, Geeta** *"Portrayal of Women in Tendulkar's Shintata Court Chalu Ahe,"* New Directions in Indian Drama. New Delhi, Prestige – 1994.

- **M. Sarat Babu** *"Vijay Tendulkar's Ghashiram Kotwal,"* A Reader's Companion, Asia book Club – New Delhi – 2003.

- **Madge V.M.-** *Vijay Tendulkar's Plays: An Anthology of Recent Criticism,* Pencraft International, 2007

- **Mehta Jay** – *Zankhi: Glimpse of Marathi Drama and Literature,* Unique offset

- **Naik M.K.** *"A History of Indian English Literature,"* Sahitya Akademi, New Delhi – 1982

- **Naik M.K. and Mokashi S. Punekar**, *Perspectives on Indian Drama in English,* Oxford UP – 1977, Madras

- **Pandey S. and Freya Barwa** – *New Directions in Indian Drama* Prestige Books.

- **Reddy, Bayapa P**. *Studies in Indian writing English with a Focus on Indian English Drama,* New Delhi: Prestige, 1990.

- **Reddy, Venkata K**. *Critical Studies in Commonwealth Literature,* New Delhi: Prestige, 1994.

- **Sarat Babu M.** – *Vijay Tendulkar's Ghashiram Kotwal,* Asia Book Club, 2003

- **Sharma Vinod Bala** *"Critical Perspectives Ghashiram Kotwal"* Asia book club-2001.

- **Sharma Vinod Bala** *"Critical Perspectives Ghasiram Kotwal",* Asia Book Club, 2001

- **Shiply Joseph J.** *Dictionary of World Literary Terms,* New Delhi: Doaba House, 1993.

- **Srinivas M.N. ,** *Social change in Modern India,* Orient Longman – 1972

- **Surendran K.V.** *"Indian Writing : Critical perspectives Sarup & Sons."* New Delhi

- **Taraporewala Freya and Pandey Sudhakar** *"Contemparary Indian Drama,"* New Delhi, Prestige Book - 1990

- **Tendulkar Vijay** *Katha* – 2001

- **Vatsyaya, Kapila**. *Traditional Indian Theatre:* Multiple Streams, New Delhi: National Book trust, 1980.

- **Veena Noble Dass** – *"Studies in Contemporary Indian Drama,"* Prestige – 1990.

# ARTICLES FROM NEWSPAPERS

- **Rajadhyaksha Mukta**, Times of India – Monday, January 29, 2007., "Times review / Book Mark., "Vijay Tendulkar answers Some questions."

- **Times News Network** "Times of India" Tuesday, May 20, 2008.

- **The Hindu** 3/10/04., The Hindu - Sunday, September 16, 2001.

# WEB SOURCES

http://www.rediff.com/news/2008/may/19vijay.htm (died article)

http://www.imdb.com/name/nm0854919/ (biography)

http://en.wikipedia.org/wiki/Vijay_Tendulkar (biography)

http://www.littleindia.com/news/123/ARTICLE/3138/2008-07-15.html (By:

Shekhar Hattangadi)

http://www.hinduonnet.com/thehindu/mag/2005/11/06/stories/2005110600310500.htm (**A rich tapestry of women's stories** ) Sunday, Nov 06, 2005 on kamala

http://salaamtheatre.org/kamala2004.html

www.urdutech.net/.../2008/05/vijaytendulkar.jpg

chat.indiatimes.com/articleshow/753698.cms

www.sajaforum.org/2008/05/obit-vijay-tend.html

http://news.bbc.co.uk/2/hi/south_asia/7407808.stm (death article)

www.hindu.com/.../stories/2007012002590800.htm (ghasiram) (Saturday, Jan 20, 2007)

http://www.hindu.com/mp/2007/01/20/images/2007012002590801.jpg

http://kpowerinfinity.spaces.live.com/Blog/cns!EEA9A8ECBFC1B50B!309.entry (((kanyadaan performance article) (August 11

Vijay Tendulkar's 'Kanyadaan' - An Unparalleled Performance)

www.indiaclub.com/shop/AuthorSelect.asp?Autho... (kanyadaan poster)

http://geekydood.wordpress.com/2008/04/30/silence-the-court-is-in-session/

http://www.quillandink.netfirms.com/Theatrecian/tcreview060506.htm (silence)

www.alibris.com/.../author/Tendulkar,%20Vijay (image)

http://timesofindia.indiatimes.com/articleshow/23796750.cms (article on ghasiram kotwal's performance) (30 Sep 2002, 2309)

http://picasaweb.google.com/suman.nsd/100MEDIA#5196466031138807074 (ghasiram kotwal)

http://www.mumbaitheatreguide.com/dramas/hindi/sakharam_binder_retold.asp (sakharam binder , performance article and photo)

http://www.sepiamutiny.com/sepia/archives/000636.html (photo sakharam binder)

http://www.iaac.us/Tendulkarfestival/VijayTendulkar.htm (photo with cast of sakharam binder)

http://www.bookrags.com/wiki/Shantata%21_Court_Chalu_Aahe (silence)

http://www.bookrags.com/wiki/Ghashiram_Kotwal

http://www.bookrags.com/wiki/Sakharam_Binder

http://www.bookrags.com/wiki/Vijay_Tendulkar

http://www.indianexpress.com/res/web/pIe/ie/daily/19991020/ile20071.html (article, Wednesday, October 20, 1999)

http://passionforcinema.com/a-conversation-with-sir-vijay-tendulkar/ (conversation with tendulkar)

http://shreevarma.homestead.com/bookreviews1.html

www.ingramcontent.com/pod-product-compliance
Lightning Source LLC
Chambersburg PA
CBHW071057280326
41928CB00050B/2546